OVERVIEW

To Dream Like God is the true story of a college professor who spends many years as an atheist, but never overcomes his uneasiness with the godless universe he has conceived. He wishes there really were a Messiah like the one Miss Irene and Miss Daphne taught him about when he was a child. He wishes it were possible to meet the Deity Whom Abraham, Isaac and Jacob met.

The professor goes on a quest for the God Who he is certain does not exist. He discovers that God uses events and stories in the pursuit of His children, just as Jesus employed signs and parables to prepare the minds of the people of His day for the coming of God. The seeker finds himself caught up in an exciting saga that stretches from the comforts of Tennessee through the wild vitality of the Amazon rain forest to the corridors outside hospital emergency rooms. The dénouement of the professor's saga teaches him the surprising lesson that God is always the One Who finds the seeker, and not the other way around.

If stories of spiritual quest appeal to you, this book may have been placed in your hands in order to advance your search. You will read in this work of a pacifist who discovers how to fight for his family; of a Romeo and Juliet who meet sixty-five years after they were separated; of what happens when a Confederate private has to decide between a MASH station and the trenches; of a young mother who earns the respect of gladiators in 203 A.D.; of a deformed baby who instructs his parents about life; of a struggling writer who discovers a unique genre, and many other stories.

The work as a whole will show you how a cold-hearted man who did not know how to love either God or his neighbor was conducted into a wonderful capacity for adoration. It will tell you how a spiritual commoner was invested with nobility. You will discover how a scholar undocks from traditional research in order to pursue the truth.

And all the stories will be incorporated into the autobiography of a former atheist who is taught to dream, not like a mere mortal, but like God.

Synopsis

To Dream Like God is the true story of a confirmed atheist who not only comes to believe in God but learns to dream the way that God dreams.

The two-volume set of *To Dream Like God* is divided into four parts, each with special characteristics organized around the central, ongoing theme of how the narrator learns to dream like God, rather than like a mere human being.

Part One (entitled "... and the Angels Laughed") recounts how the narrator, a university professor firmly entrenched in his atheism, is led to know God through adventures which take place during a journey between two locations, the Amazon rain forest of Brazil and a modern university city in the southern United States. This volume displays how the Gospel supersedes theism in order to carry the narrator to heights he could never have conceived when he began his journey.

Part Two (entitled "The Eloquence of God") tells six stories which detail ways in which God works in the daily lives of people whom the narrator meets. These accounts reveal God's nature and His plans to remarkable people who at first do not suspect that God is actively plotting their destiny. This part demonstrates the fashion in which God employs the language of event to regenerate and inspire individuals mired in the commonplaces of everyday life and relationships.

Part Three (entitled "Annals of Brokenness & Glory") shows the manner in which God teaches the former atheist to deal with his fears, how to love and be loved, and how to aspire to a life of splendor, rather than remain in the mediocrity which is his natural habitat. This section carries the narrator deeper and deeper into the mysteries of Christ, and of death and human destiny.

Part Four (entitled "The Dream of God") takes the entire series to its conclusion. The glory of Christ's final Victory is displayed to the one-time atheist, and his life is fulfilled as he is commissioned to play an exciting role in hastening that Victory. The narrator finally learns to dream as God dreams!

The collection's purpose is to appeal to unbelievers in Christ's sense of "believe" at the same time that it strengthens believers. This splendid spiritual autobiography shows how God has spoken through the idiom of event and story to the World and to the author.

⊱⊰⊱⊰⊱⊰⊱⊰⊱⊰

To Dream Like God
by Yulan Washburn

Volume I

PART ONE
... And the Angels Laughed

PART TWO
The Eloquence of God

Volume II

PART THREE
Annals of Brokenness & Glory

PART FOUR
The Dream of God

... *And the Angels*

Laughed

♌♌♌♌♌♌

PART ONE

of

To Dream Like God

Published by William and Warren, Inc.
1200 Paint Rock Road
Kingston, Tennessee 37763

Library of Congress Cataloging-in-Publication Data
Washburn, Yulan;

    ISBN 0-9652007-4-4
    1. Non-fiction
    2. Biography
    3. Religion

Dewey System — Non-fiction: Short Stories

Cover and text design by Debbie Patrick, Knoxville, Tennessee
Printed in Thailand

Readers interested in seeing pictures of many of the people and places which appear in *To Dream Like God* (Amazonian scenes, Garlan and Helen, Sarah and Lowell, Mildred, Up Home, etc.) may do so by going to the book's website at:

www.todreamlikegod.com

In memory of

The Rev. Tom Griffiths,
Mumbles Baptist Church
Swansea, Wales
"Someday we will understand"

Yn awr, gweld mewn drych yr ydym, a hynny'n aneglur;
ond yna cawn weld wyneb
yn wyneb.

1 Cor 13 : 12a
(in Welsh, 'the language of Heaven')

⊱⊰⊱⊰⊱⊰⊱⊰⊱⊰

Introduction:
THE GOSPEL GENRE

This book is the story of my quest for God and some of the surprises and discoveries to which the quest has led me.

The greatest surprise the quest has provided me is that God seeks fellowship with His children even more eagerly than we search for Him. The most significant discovery provided me has been that God uses many kinds of expression to conduct His fellowship, and that one of the chief expressions, as the Gospels illustrate so clearly, is story itself.

In fact, the word "Gospel" has in the course of my fellowship with God come to have very special meanings. For me, it refers first to a particular type of narrative, stories in which God comes unbidden into the lives of His children to enable them to reach their highest destiny. The books which we call "The Gospels," those brief works of Matthew, Mark, Luke and John, are made up of tales of little people—widows with mites, carpenters on a trip with pregnant wives, fishermen mending their nets on the sand, and mothers with dead sons—to whom God through Christ demonstrated that they mattered supremely to Him as He passed by quickly, His very shadow changing their lives forever.

Secondly, the Gospel signifies that God loves us, and love by its nature demands personal contact, life-giving interaction between those who hold one another in highest regard. God is not distant and silent. He comes to us. We often do not respond to His initiatives, do not allow ourselves to recognize His bright and rich languages. But it is His wish that we know Him and enjoy His nearness.

Thirdly, the Gospel teaches that God honors us by calling us in Christ to join Him in the stupendous enterprise of refashioning the nature of reality. He calls us to dream His dream and act upon it. Death, sin, pain and sorrow will be stricken by Jesus Christ from human existence, and we are called to play a committed role in the elimination of these plagues upon life.

The stories in this volume have their roots in the same Gospel Genre which the New Testament writers introduced to the world. One aspect of that Gospel—the Second Coming or the final Victory of Christ—is made preeminent in these pages, but all of the stories included are based on God's entry into the lives of unremarkable people, people who are then made remarkable by His entry.

It is important to keep in mind as you read the following stories that they are all based on real life. Except for the "Dreaming in Carthage" chapter, which deals with Perpetua, a young woman who was martyred in 203 A.D., I know personally most of the people depicted in these pages and have witnessed the changes which took place in their lives. I have at times altered names and jumbled details to protect privacy or focus meaning, but the selections included emerge largely from my own experience.

And these stories, in a fashion which remains mysterious to me, have played a central role in elaborating my own story, the account not only of the way I came to God, but of the way Christ comes to me and guides me. They display what has happened to me because of His entry into my heart, entry forced at times by means of individuals and events which at first did not appear to have any relation whatsoever to Christ or His action.

The purpose of this collection is to encourage its readers as I myself have been encouraged by the fellowship of story. If such dramas and comedies as these can vivify the Gospel in the life of a person as unextraordinary as I, then similar stories are coalescing in the lives of my readers, if they will but see the pattern. Life is so hard, death is always so near, and love is often so hard to come by, within ourselves and from others, that we require encouragement.

God's kindness is always as near as our breath. We do not have to labor our way to Him. He is constantly with us. Our task is to learn His language, which makes glorious sense of everything, good and bad, which befalls us, and calls us beyond the horizons to which merely human image and utterance bind us.

We have been created so that we can indeed, in our very limited way, dream like God and enact His limitless dreams into the world around us.

For people like me, and perhaps you, the language of sacred dream is learned at the deepest level through event and story, not through texts or discourses couched in proposition and exposition. The accounts which follow relate several ways in which God has narrated His presence into my life and the lives of people who have affected me.

PART ONE

... And the Angels Laughed

THE QUEST
And Its Results:

*(The story of a young man who goes on a quest for God
and encounters a surprise)*

Holy Atheism

The Jungle

The Day of the Dead

Lessons in Creaturehood

The Quest

The God Who Comes

and

AFTERMATH:
The Fellowship of Story

*(What happens to the quester as his story issues
in even more unexpected results)*

THE QUEST
And Its Results:

PREAMBLE

I cannot prove to you that angels laugh, but Christian scripture several times portrays them in a state of jubilation, and it is on the authority of the Lord Jesus that we know they rejoice when even a single soul is saved.

My own life suggests to me that laughter must be one of the pet expressions of angels. Some of them have to be very close to what we earthlings would call comedians.

I won't presume that I have often heard their glee first hand, but I am certain that I would have done so on many occasions, had I been discerning enough to listen.

Holy Atheism

I grew up in Charlotte, North Carolina. Although my father was a Baptist preacher's kid, my parents rarely attended church. They said they believed in God and Jesus, but for some reason they never wanted to go to worship services.

I *did* want to go to worship.

And I went. On my own, with no forcing. By the time I was eight, I either rode a bus or walked three miles downtown to the First Baptist Church. At that age, of course, I didn't really understand religion, but something called me to go to church. I enjoyed the stories about Abraham and Moses and Ruth, and I attended Sunday School every week to hear about them. During preaching—which is what we called the worship service—I would sit up in the balcony by myself or with a little friend, and I would idly draw pictures on the bulletin and listen, taking in as much as I could from the sermons.

Because I went to a Baptist church, I acquired a vague sense that baptism by immersion was highly important. My childish mind of course couldn't expound baptism's spiritual purpose, but I picked up enough to know it was something I needed to do.

"You want to become a member of the family, don't you?" was how C.C. Warren, the pastor, kindly put it when I went to talk to him. He questioned me a bit, quite respectfully as I recall, and then, with that understanding which great Baptist pastors have that children often know things they don't even know they know, gave me his blessing.

So one Sunday morning, I went down front when they sang the invitational hymn at the end of the service. "Just as I Am," all four verses, with repetitions, and I took everything I had to offer, my eight year old little self and my presence, and I stood before the congregation for them to vote whether they would accept me. The church secretary, a nice lady, had me fill out a little white card with my name and address, and a box to check if I was coming by letter, transfer, or baptism. Dr. Warren asked me if I knew that I was a sinner and that Jesus had died for me. I didn't understand much, but I knew even at that age that, somehow and in some way, I needed saving, so I was honest as only a child can be when I said yes.

The next Sunday I was baptized. My parents came to see their son appear in the maroon curtained baptistry with a scene of palm trees by the River Jordan painted across the back wall. It was one of the few times I recall being in church with my folks. My Sunday School teacher dressed me in a kind of white choir robe, 'way too big and long. I must have looked a little like Dopey of the Seven Dwarfs as I entered the pool. I remember that Dr. Warren helpfully took my hand to help me wade through the water, which was, to me, lake level, up to my chest. I also remember the big, awesome congregation of several hundred people out there witnessing us, and I searched for my parents in the pews. Dr. Warren held a handkerchief to my nose so I wouldn't choke, and laid me back in the pool, signifying my death and rebirth in Christ. I came up out of the water, gasping and blinking at the faces before me. A lot of them were smiling.

When I was going up the steps of the baptismal pool, I stumbled, and my Sunday School teacher reached out and steadied me. The cold wet robe was plastered to my skin, and I was embarrassed that everybody in that congregation could see my little boy's skinny backside outlined under the white cotton cloth as I disappeared from their view. My mother cried, and my father was proud.

As I said, I did not really know what things were all about on that morning I gave my heart to Christ. I was a puny, unprofitable addition to His Body, but I am sure that somewhere above that sanctuary, angel chuckle could be heard by those saints at First Baptist Church who were equipped to hear it.

At eleven or twelve I got my first job as a paperboy with The Charlotte News. The newspaper was honoring all its carriers, putting their photograph on the front page of the second section, with a little seven line article about each of us. I felt so important when my turn came. The reporter who interviewed me asked, "What do you want to be when you grow up?"

"A preacher," I told him with pride.

When I was sixteen, a major event derailed my ambition to serve God: I became an atheist, a full-fledged 20th century unbeliever.

I was interested in books and I admired authors. It dawned on me that few of the Writing Class which I was encountering believed in God, and none that I could find believed in C.C. Warren's Father, Son and Holy Ghost, in whose names I had been immersed. That started me doubting Warren and his Bible, and my doubt soon became certainty that all theism was an imposture. Some people tell me that they believe there is no such thing as an atheist, but I can testify that I really came to believe that God did not exist. I wasn't at all happy with the way I saw things, but it truly seemed to me that there was no god, C.C. Warren's or anybody else's.

I was troubled. I was sad. I envied people who claimed to have faith in God, in the divinity of Jesus. I wanted to believe as they believed, but I just could not. Young as I was, I knew what the stakes were, what a godless universe meant about death, that after death there was nothingness. I also figured out what a godless world meant about morality. It meant that nothingness extended into the realm of right and wrong. There was no such thing as good and evil. I came to the conclusion that all moral preference came merely from our desires and pleasures, and that conscience and guilt were products exuded by our brains in the same fashion that sweat was exuded from our armpits.

Worse, I also came to believe that what we called love did not exist. Love was an illusion, a human concoction, another secretion of our cerebrum, and no more momentous than our toenails or earwax. We human beings had dressed love in the gala costumes which our cultures had provided for us, in much the same manner as culture had provided robes and head scarves for Arabs and Brooks Brothers suits and striped ties for dwellers of Manhattan. The herd instinct perhaps was real. Love was not.

I detested the way I saw the world. I kept going to churches off and on for the next several years, hoping I would come to have faith in God. I sought God in books and tried every alternative I could find, but belief in Him was an impossibility for me. There was no God.

I arrived somewhat bitterly at the conclusion that people who did believe did so only because they had been raised that way. Christianity and Islam and Buddhism were at best no more than systems thrown up by complex social and historical forces. At worst, religions were some sort of crutch for those who could not face the cold, spiritually empty universe we inhabited.

My life went on. I married—that was the first time my disbelief in love was challenged. I studied. I read all the books one is supposed to read. I earned an undergraduate degree in English and philosophy from one fine university, a Master's in foreign languages from another admired institution, and a Ph.D. from one of the highest ranked university departments in the United States. I received the best that education had to offer.

Throughout those years, I never ceased to seek the God I was certain did not exist. I profoundly wanted to believe in the loving Father whom Jesus had so beautifully characterized. But I knew in my own mind, beyond any reasonable doubt, that He didn't exist, and that poor Jesus's bones had lain hidden under the dust of Palestine for two thousand years.

Twenty years went by. I devoted myself to my academic career, and great modern literature became the passion of my life. I did not fail to notice wryly that none of the writers I studied was a practicing Baptist. Most of my academic colleagues shared roughly the spiritual views I held. Few would have disagreed with my theory that Jesus of Nazareth lay in the same crust of earth which consumed the bones of Dante, Cervantes and Shakespeare, and that it was wondrous that their visions had survived the fate of their bodies. I never entirely gave up my search to overturn my own theory of godlessness, but it held me fast. I kept my quest a secret, of course. I wanted to be a member of the academic family, and I carefully observed the house rules and taboos.

Life, in many ways, was good. I taught history and literature, Spanish and French. I traveled. I joined the fraternity of writers by publishing a few articles and a book. My wife and I had two daughters. When I was in my mid thirties, we were sent to the University of Wisconsin for me to do a summer's postdoctoral work in Portuguese. I was in intensive language classes from early in the morning till mid afternoon week after week. My family and I canoed the lakes of Madison and went to Milwaukee's zoo. It was a lovely time.

I was called out of class one day by a long distance call from my university.

"How would you like to go to the Brazilian Amazon as a Visiting Professor of American Civilization?"

My wife and I batted around the offer of a semester in the Amazon. I wanted to go to London or Paris, Rome or Madrid—some place where the major writers of Western Culture had lived and worked. But the jungle? That wasn't my idea of how to pursue literary studies. Eventually my wife and I persuaded one another that living in a city in the midst of the rain forest would be a great, once-in-a-lifetime adventure.

Our families reacted in typical ways. My mother cried and my father was proud. My energetic mother-in-law, a staunch Southern Baptist, disconcerted me by securing from her Foreign Mission Board the names of several missionaries living in Manaus, the city where we would be stationed. My wife, whom (I feared) I had helped turn into as much of an unbeliever as I was, wrote the missionaries as a favor to her insistent mother, letting them know we were coming. I was dubious about the matter but figured, "What harm can it do?"

The angels went wild with laughter.

The Jungle

I will never forget waking up at six in the morning on a September day and looking out of the airplane window. It was my first view of the rain forest, a vast ocean of green flowing beneath us endlessly as the jet began its long descent into Manaus. The jungle was laced with bright rivers, the widest I had ever seen, and as we settled nearer the earth for our final approach over the tall trees, I could make out boats in the water and villages on the margins of the rivers.

I expected a delegation from the University of Amazonas to meet their new professor at the airport. What I did not know as my wife and our two little daughters gathered their carry-ons from underneath the seats and the bins overhead was that one of those angels which I was certain was a myth had monkeyed with the communications system between my university and the city of Manaus. The university delegates of Amazonas were still sleeping. Not one of them had an inkling that we were arriving that morning.

When we deplaned onto the tarmac under Amazonia's early morning sunlight, we were greeted by a small horde of Southern Baptist missionaries and their families, smiling and waving. Only they had received word that we were arriving.

I was chagrined. If there was anything I didn't want to do at that point in my life, it was to pal around with a bunch of fundamentalist American missionaries!

The missionaries conducted us in several cars to an English style hotel in the center of the city. When we drove up in front of the hotel, which was called The Lord, the first irony of our great adventure completely escaped me, but how those pesky angels must have grinned at the way every detail of our adventure was being carefully prepared!

Things began to go wrong from the first. Prices in Manaus were astronomical. The Lord Hotel, even though it was the most reasonably priced decent accommodation in the city, was well beyond our modest budget. The housing situation was appalling. Nothing furnished was available. University colleagues took us house hunting, but every place we looked at had jungle prices of three or four times the rate that we could pay. Money was flowing out of our pockets alarmingly in the hotel.

We were soon in a sad state. I got frighteningly ill from the hectic pace of apartment hunting in Amazonian heat. With me prostrate, my wife fell into a depression and lay awake at night sobbing over where she would find a pediatrician if our children also came down with an illness. Our gentle seven year old daughter, Nan, was totally freaked by the strangeness of her surroundings. She shivered at the common Amazonian stories of alligators and spiders and giant boa constrictors. When a benign waiter in the Lord restaurant offered her more food, asking, *Mais?* (a word pronounced just like the English word for a tiny rodent), she thought he was offering her a mouse, and refused to eat anything but peanut butter sandwiches for days thereafter. Our ten year old daughter Ginny was mightily bored, demanding when all the adventure she had been promised was going to start.

The missionaries came to our rescue. Natural born improvisers because of the nature of their lives, they proposed a solution to the problem of house furnishings. They rounded up a couch, a few chairs, a table, two beds from their own homes. They took us to a place where we could buy a tiny Japanese refrigerator, which we could resell when we left. Their wives found a double burner hot plate to use in our kitchen. They convinced Ginny and me that we would be able to sleep in hammocks, like most natives of Amazonia did.

That still left the problem of a place to live. When we were at our lowest point, sure that no apartment within our reach existed in Manaus, and that my wife and children would have to return alone to the United States, a miracle occurred. A family named Barbosa, somehow hearing of our plight, offered us an apartment of four clean, airy, affordable rooms on the ground floor of their house, just blocks from my university classroom and central to all the shops. It was perfect! Moreover, Dr. Barbosa, it turned out, was a pediatrician, and his office was situated along the hallway which led from the main entrance of the building to our front patio. My anxious wife found herself installed in a pleasant home with a live-in pediatrician.

The angels must have laughed in delight at how things were unfolding.

There was still culture shock to deal with, especially for middle-class innocents like ourselves, accustomed to all the advantages of an industrially advanced nation. Manaus was a city which had just passed through a long depression. Old mansions which had once been elegant were now dilapidated and in need of repair. Everywhere we looked, buildings which pretended to be white were blotched with dark jungle fungus. Hundreds of thousands of poverty-stricken people had moved into the city, hoping for a better life as the new Free Trade Zone developed. Many of them lived in the most degrading misery. Huge buzzards circled in the sky overhead, fluttering down to eat the smelly refuse which was thrown on the sidewalks. Our trips through the city on errands or to accept invitations from the hospitable Brazilians left us sad and pensive about the sights we saw.

Even in our first-rate quarters, everyday life had its trials. We were at first intimidated by the lizards which lived on the walls and ceilings of our apartment. In time, we became grateful for the way they kept down the number of flies, and each reptile seemed to take on a personality all its own.

We cheered one night when we saw a fly light on the wall and walk straight into a crack in the door frame where we knew one of the lizards was waiting. Still, it was a bit unnerving to take a shower with bright eyes staring at you from cracks in the tiles, or to feel a little body slither across your hand when you reached into a dark room to turn on the lights before you entered. Fat cockroaches whizzed through the open windows at night when I tried to read or write, smacking into the wall beside my lamp, plopping on their broad backs in the middle of the page in front of me, legs flailing wildly under the glare of the lamp.

We missed our families terribly. A generous ham radio operator allowed us to call the United States every Monday night at nine o'clock. If the weather was clear and an operator in the United States picked us up, we would be patched through by telephone for a collect call to our loved ones. Such contact helped, but it was chancy, and those ghostly voices of our relatives and friends coming thousands of miles over short wave could never fully relieve our sense of loneliness and isolation.

Life in Manaus was especially hard on my wife, who was obliged to keep home and family going under circumstances something like those which her grandmothers had endured. She daily boiled the water we would use and twice weekly she filled a concrete trough on the back patio with cold, slightly muddy water piped untreated from the river and scrubbed our clothes till her hands were red and aching. Since her kitchen had few conveniences, she fed us lots of bananas and scrambled eggs, and she helped the kids learn to tolerate the British milk substitute which was the only kind that would stay fresh in the heat. Every trip for groceries was an adventure for her. The goods she found on the shelves depended on what the last river freighter had brought in, and sometimes the shelves were empty of even commonplace items. When the kids complained about the food, she poked cloves into a rectangle of canned Spam and helped us pretend we were having Thanksgiving. She would hear one morning that a cargo of frozen chickens had just arrived from Puerto Rico, and she would rush down to the markets to get us a feast before the hoarders had bought them all up. Since she knew little Portuguese, things occasionally got difficult. She never figured out a way to tell a helpful clerk that she preferred another bag of beans because the one he had given her was crawling with vermin. In the midst of such trials, she home schooled our children and was a miracle worker at finding amusements for them.

My own work life was extremely stimulating. My Portuguese advanced amazingly. I made lists every day of words I did not know, I studied grammar, I sought every opportunity to be with Brazilians in different situations. In time, I was invited to give talks to local groups, and I even wrote a series of articles for one of the newspapers. I met with regional poets and writers. Best of all, I loved teaching American literature to eager Brazilian students.

We saw the missionaries occasionally, but for the most part we went about our business and they went about theirs. They were busy, and so were we.

Just as we were getting adjusted to the climate, and things seemed to be leveling off into a smooth routine, we were hit by another crisis. My monthly paycheck failed to arrive from the United States. From what I now know about how Heaven operates, I am guessing that one of the more nerdy angels was responsible, tinkering unconscionably with transfers in the international banking network.

At first we assumed some minor glitch had occurred, that the money would arrive momentarily. Every day I went to the Banco de Londres to check our balance. Our nervousness soon grew into full-fledged panic. We sent urgent messages to the States. Curt answers came back that the university had indeed sent the money, why was I complaining? A courteous but firm teller in the Banco de Londres informed me that I could draw no more funds.

We were totally broke. The Barbosa's rent was unpaid, and we had nothing left for food. A day or two more and the bananas were gone and the peanut butter jar scoured. I knew no one at the University of Amazonas well enough to cadge a loan. After a desperate family conference, we scraped together the coins we had left, just enough for me to take a taxi across town to see Richard, one of the missionaries.

When I went up to the door of Richard's house and clapped my hands (that's how you "knock" in the Amazon), I am sure the angels were also clapping their palms in glee. I had barely begun my embarrassed explanation of our situation to Richard when he stopped me and plopped the equivalent of a couple of hundred U.S. dollars in Brazilian *cruzeiros* down on the kitchen table in front of me. It was years later before it occurred to me to wonder what Richard, a relatively poor missionary, was doing with so much money on his person that day. I doubt that he himself really knew the reason he had the money until the moment I began babbling about lost paychecks, but I suspect that an angel was chuckling knowingly in the background, and that Richard probably knew it, even though he said nothing to me.

From that day on we spent more and more time with the missionaries. I confess that at first I did it almost cynically, feeling vaguely I owed them attention for all their help. As time went on I finally admitted to myself that I liked being with the Baptists because they were interesting, big-hearted people. They were helping everybody, not just me.

We attended services (for cultural reasons, I told myself) in the little churches which the missionaries were establishing. For the first time we met humble Brazilians of the peasant or working class, splendid people who received our family with kindness and a sometimes overwhelming curiosity. Brazilian children would line up in the pew behind us to stare fascinated at the backs of our daughters' heads, and my wife shook hands with countless adults who wanted to be her friend, but with whom she could not exchange a word intelligible to either of them.

I was strangely affected by the religious services. I heard hymns that I used to hear at First Baptist in Charlotte, but this time they were sung by dark, enthusiastic people of a dazzling mixture of races and social classes. I realized with a shock that the sacred music and the harmonies were beautiful and that the words were not at all trite, as I had come to suppose. Somehow, because the words of the hymns were in Portuguese, I could hear their message as if for the first time. Meanings which would have been inconceivable to me in the United States resonated deep inside as I listened or joined in the singing.

Once I sat in the back of a white stuccoed chapel with no glass in the windows. Birds were flying in and out as the organ played, and Richard delivered a message which would have been quite familiar in revivals back at the church of my childhood. I looked around at the setting and the earnest Indian and Negro and European faces, and I was plunged into sadness. All this, as I saw things, would soon come to an end. These people in this backwater of civilization still responded to the old verities of Christianity, but I was aware that a tide of which I was a part had risen against them back in the developed countries.

God was dead, and not just because the madman Nietzsche had declared Him to be so, and Altizer had popularized the madman's ravings. The primitive notion of Yahweh had been washed away by a flood of science and knowledge, by modernity and industrialization. These jungle people and their foreign missionaries did not realize it, but the stately old ship of traditional Christianity was going down, like everything else that was traditional. Christianity was already bow up in the universities and government, in the cinemas and publishing houses, in fact in all the places that really counted in the carrying forward of modern civilization. There was no God! Jesus's bones were moldering in Palestine!

As I once listened to *Blessed Assurance* in Portuguese, I began to weep. How splendid all this was! I had never been able to see its loveliness in my own country. First Baptist and First Presbyterian and First Methodist, all these churches, with their people and songs and celebrations, their funerals and weddings and preaching had had something beautiful and profound about them, and I had missed out on the loveliness and depth. And it was now all fading before my eyes, all except this anachronism in the jungle. In fifty years the church houses I knew back home would be empty, the church yards I saw in the countryside off our highways would be abandoned and unkept. These little chapels in the rain forest would inevitably follow suit. The day of Jesus Christ and His church was over. What a loss!

I looked through my tears at the children earnestly singing, at the creased brown faces of the very old hovering over their Portuguese Bibles, at the cheerful countenance of my new missionary friends, all absorbed in their vanishing myth. If only the myth had been true!

So I thought as I went, time after time, to services in a decaying city in the rain forest.

The angels must have been in an upheaval of delight! I was on the verge of my first touch of Glory.

The Day of the Dead

When Richard issued an invitation to go down the Amazon River with him on an all day mission trip, I was excited. I did not know what a "mission trip" was, but I was not about to resist the chance of a fifteen hour river journey through the wild interior I had heard so much about.

Had I been sensitive, I would have seen from the outset that the whole trip that day wore the aspect of a bizarre theatrical production, staged by the Creator Himself. Images from it burn in my mind like fire to this moment.

Accompanied by a few Brazilian members of Richard's church, my daughter Ginny and I boarded a little blue and white cabin cruiser at dawn on November second, the Day of the Dead in Brazil. The craft floated down an *igarapé* past the Manaus slaughter house in the soft early morning light. Flocks of buzzards circled overhead, and some of the bolder ones landed to quarrel viciously over scraps which had been flung into the mire of the stockyard on the edge of the water.

Soon we were going down the Rio Negro, a two-mile wide river whose waters mysteriously appear as black as ebony. Within half an hour our little boat was bouncing in the turbulence of the spectacular Meeting of the Waters, the confluence where the currents of the Rio Negro collide with the milk chocolate rush of the Solimões to form the Amazon itself. We sailed roughly east through the jungle, with many bends and turns that had us facing every point of the compass at one time or the other in our journey.

The Amazon River itself, once we entered it, was several miles wide, and I got to see some of the famous floating islands, huge chunks of earth which the powerful current had chewed from the banks upstream. I had read back in Madison, Wisconsin that such islands, some containing fair-sized trees, were so large that they would float for days down river until they dissolved and sank into the depths of the river. The Brazilians on board told me they had sometimes seen desperate cattle or wild animals trapped on such islands, caught by surprise when the plot where they were grazing or feeding toppled into the river.

Several hours went by as we steadily plowed our way downstream under the growing heat of the morning sun. Along the edges of the river I saw occasional clearings, with a solitary house facing the river. They were unpainted wood structures on stilts, bleached gray by equatorial sunlight. All of them seemed to have Dutch doors, with the bottom half closed to keep young children from wandering outside, or creatures from the outside from entering. Once or twice a mother with a naked baby in her arms appeared in the upper portion of a doorway and waved a salute at our boat. Beside the houses, washing flapped in the breeze, and some of the yards featured spectacular flower plots in red, yellow and orange.

As the morning advanced, the sun blazed hotter and brighter, blinding us with its brilliant reflections off the brown water. Flocks of parakeets crossed the wide expanse and made a racket overhead. Great white herons majestically and cautiously stepped their way through the shallow waters near shore. I was once startled as a pair of large pink dolphins crashed to the surface beside our boat, splashing the deck. They followed us playfully for some time, either for company or in hopes of food thrown overboard.

I dominated the thrills of nervousness I occasionally felt. I realized we were traveling deep in the middle of a virtually uninhabited wilderness. I had been told that an old-fashioned drafter's compass could be set on a map of Brazil, with its point on Manaus, and a thousand mile circle traced. Within that circumference, there was almost nothing but jungle. Scattered *caboclos* (white/Indian mix breeds) and tribes of Indians eked out a living on the banks of the Amazon and its tributaries, and there were a few towns and logging camps, but the interior was mostly wild, some of it never fully explored.

There were diversions. The Brazilians cooked up a rice and beans lunch while we maintained our course. My daughter Ginny noticed black specks in the rice. "Brazilian pepper?" I asked one of the Brazilians. My companion, his mouth full of food, smiled.

"*Bicho*," he responded, and forked in a mouthful. "Just a few bugs." I saw everyone else digging in with gusto, so I did too.

Once we pulled up to a simple pier to meet a young woman who was going to lead the singing of hymns. Since she had not arrived from her trek down the jungle paths from her village, Richard decided to take advantage of the delay to fish. I had heard there were 200 pound *pirarucus* in the river. What I didn't know was that there were catfish also, but nothing like the ten-ounce ones I had been proud to catch on Brushy Creek back in North Carolina. Richard baited his hook, and his first strike was a hard fighting thirty-five pound cat. Richard and the excited Brazilians just had time to skin the monster and put it on ice before the song leader showed up.

The little boat then set out for its final destination, a cemetery on the opposite shore of the Amazon. While the Brazilians practiced their hymns, the craft labored across the miles of open water. In the middle of what appeared to be the vast lake on which we traveled, the sun was scorching and bright, and I sought the shade of the cabin.

After a time I could see the distant bank begin to rise imposingly. The Amazon actually is a vast, very flat basin. There is little change in elevation—less than fifty feet—from the bottom of the Andes to the Atlantic Ocean. The hill looming in front of our prow was a rare sight. On this rise, I could see that the forest had been cleared, and soon I could make out a white fence.

As we drew within the shadow of the hill, we passed several forty foot long dugout canoes. Other dugouts filled with families skimmed through the water from nearby tributaries. I could understand why this modest promontory had been chosen as the site for a graveyard. It was the only place for miles around high enough to be safe from the seasonal floods which powerfully washed the banks of the Amazon system. As far as I could tell, there was no access to the cemetery except by water. There certainly were no roads this deep in the jungle.

The Baptists slowly pulled in to shore and moored at a tree a hundred yards upriver from the cemetery. They unpacked a little loudspeaker and attached it to a car battery in the shade of the tree. The song leader assembled the half dozen boat people into a semicircle, and the tiny choir began to sing hymns. Richard later would preach. Several boxes of tracts rested nearby for distribution later.

I didn't know whether I wanted to be associated with such goings-on. Richard understood, and tolerantly encouraged me to take my camera to the cemetery. "I'll bet you've never seen anything like it," he said.

He was right. Somehow, despite all my studies, I had never run into what the Day of the Dead meant in Brazil. As I made my way to the top of the hill and along the fence, I found that the bank side before the gate was crowded with people, all dressed in more or less poor finery. Down below, scores of dugouts were pulled up on shore, and others were arriving and leaving. It was like some kind of great open-air market place, very colorful and busy.

I felt awkward and out of place, but a toothless man greeted me cordially, and a young woman in a print dress flashed me a brilliant smile. One or two people carrying little sacks put down their burdens and came over to shake my hand. I found that these people of the interior were as interested in the American who spoke Portuguese as he was in them. I discovered that they came to this cemetery once a year to take care of the resting places of their dead. The bags contained clean sand, white stones and colored shells. They would pour the sand to build up the mounds of the graves and line them with stones and other ornaments.

When I accompanied a young family through the entrance, I was astonished. Around a large white plaster cross just inside the gate, hundreds, perhaps thousands of snowy tapers burned. So many candles had already melted that the foot of the cross and a wide area around it were covered by a glacier of thick layers of wax, probably from this year and years past. The smell of the tallow was almost overpowering.

The cemetery yard contained several dozen graves, which seemed very few to me for a regional graveyard until I learned that Brazilians use the same grave over and over. As the remains of one occupant decay, the grave site is re-employed again and again.

I wandered up and down the rows, reading the simple inscriptions, usually a name and a date. Some of the crosses were of plaster, some weathered wood, with the cross arm bound in place by tough twine. I was shocked that the majority of the tombs were those of babies and little children.

I at first wondered about the propriety of taking photographs, but I quickly learned that everyone wanted me to take their picture. They seemed proud to have a foreigner with them, and they were eager to have the record of this day and their lost loved ones go out into the world beyond the rivers where many of them had spent their entire lives. I found that some of them had never seen a car, or even a paved street.

As I moved around and watched family members working to beautify the graves and tombs, a lone jet plane, passing so high overhead that it made no sound, left a long vapor trail in the afternoon sky.

At first the exoticism of the scene was paramount in my mind, but soon the reality of what was taking place began to grip me. Mothers stoically knelt on the rough ground beside tiny, neat mounds, carefully arranging the white stones and shells in pretty patterns. Men grunted as they shoveled sand. Fathers, mothers, grandparents, little ones—the dead were being remembered and cared for.

I could hear the murmur of Richard's voice, preaching in the background in his accented but supple Portuguese about salvation and the resurrection.

As the sun began to descend, the cemetery slowly emptied. People wanted to paddle to their villages or houses before darkness covered the river.

The little group of Baptists loaded up their paraphernalia, and we embarked. After dropping off our song leader, our boat hugged the south bank of the river for some time and then turned its prow across the Amazon to the other bank which, I was told, was about eight miles away. Somehow, because of the way the river looped, our course carried us directly into the orange ball of the sun, hung like a vast Christmas ornament over the shimmering water. If we journeyed fast enough and long enough, it appeared, the prow of our boat must surely puncture it.

Tired, all our minds filled with images of our day, we were silent as we plowed against the current toward Manaus. The upstream trip would take several hours, and the motors were laboring.

Evening descended, and shortly after six o'clock as black a darkness as I had ever seen settled upon us. Stars burst out, filling the heavens. Their light was so brightly clear that for the first time since I was a child I felt I could reach out and touch the constellations.

An hour and a half out of Manaus, the Brazilians and Richard decided they had made good enough time that they could stop and fish for an hour or so. The boat's searchlight felt its way along the riverbank until the pilot discovered a small cove. We pulled in and anchored a hundred yards off shore. Gear was brought out, and soon the quiet, contented fishermen were whirring and splashing.

My mind was so full of I knew not what that I did not accept the invitation to fish. I climbed on top of the cabin and sat down to rehearse the day, sprawling my legs over the boat's windscreen. The stars were twinkling in the blackness. There was no wind. Except for the lap of water against the hull and an occasional exclamation from the fishermen as they cast their lures into the darkness, there was no sound.

My mind teemed with images of the day. After some time I became aware that the night was not so noiseless as I had first thought. I began to pay close attention. A racket was rising in intensity around me. I thought I could hear animals thrashing about on shore. It was as if innumerable creatures of various sizes were crawling through the undergrowth, forcing aside bushes, snapping branches, trampling reeds. The shore in this cove was being disturbed by an enormous commotion.

I commented on it to a companionable Brazilian who had tired of fishing—no more thirty-five pound catfish, evidently—and was lounging beside me. He chuckled at my innocence.

"Não são animais. É a vegetação. 'Tá crescendo."

"That's not animals," he was saying. "It's the vegetation increasing. The plants grow during the night. The sound you hear is the swelling of life in the leaves and stems. The branches sway and weave, crackle and snap against one another all night long. That's the power of the rain forest."

I was shocked. I couldn't believe him. He insisted.

I remembered all of a sudden a time shortly after we had first come to Manaus. My family and I stood at the rail of the hotel roof balcony. From the perspective of the Lord Hotel, we looked out over a sprawling city of three-quarters of a million people. From that height we could see the limits of Manaus, where the city ended and the jungle began. We were totally encircled by green. As I stood beside my family, I shivered, remembering pictures taken from the air of lost Mayan cities, once large and well populated as was Manaus, but now deserted and repossessed by the Central American jungle.

If what my companion said was even half true, then human beings had to labor daily against that green wall fringing Manaus, or it would creep inexorably inward and, within a relatively short time, reclaim the streets and buildings of the city. Without constant human effort and enterprise, Manaus would be within a few years as lost as the ancient cities of the Mayans. The upper stories of ruined hotels and office buildings jutting above the expanse of jungle would be the only sign that the Free Trade Zone and university city had ever existed.

In a blinding flash, on top of that boat returning from a mission trip, my whole vision of life was spinning out of control. Where I came from, we considered nature to be basically benign. She might trouble us occasionally with electrical storms during the summer and crop failure every decade or so, but generally she sustained human life quite predictably, harvest after harvest. Nature was a place to which we retreated for refreshment. We went to her to hike, to camp and relax, to build a fire and roast marshmallows.

On this night the sparkling stars above burned into my mind like lightening bolts. As I listened to the smack of water against the side of the boat and heard the crackling and popping on shore of the plants' surging vitality, a terrible image floated between me and the stars.

I saw my planet incinerated by the death and explosion of the sun. Earth was floating, a huge piece of slag, in the cold, silent darkness of the universe. Freezing winds swept over it, and into my vision, white pieces of paper which had somehow survived the final holocaust were being swept across the barren surface, pages of Shakespeare and Dante and Cervantes. No life was left to read them. They blew and tumbled, useless and forsaken, from one side of the waterless, lightless planet to the other. No other thing of humankind remained.

I was overcome with awe. I wanted to weep. For the first time, I realized that I had spent all my life, like tonight, on something human beings had made, or in something we had created, or beside something we had constructed or on my way to something we had conceived. Without knowing it, I had absorbed the message that man was in control. Humankind ruled.

We were the center and measure of all things. This was the medium within which I lived, this was the basic lesson of my life, and I never even knew that I had learned it.

All of a sudden, my feet dangling over the windshield and with fishermen around me, I recognized that the message I had so trustingly swallowed was a lie. Mankind ruled and controlled very little. We were guests on the planet. We were in the universe on sufferance. Without constant effort on our part, without constant luck, our mightiest efforts would be swallowed back into nature in the same way that the jungle had absorbed the Mayan sacred cities, and the desert sands had reclaimed Nineveh and Babylon and the other great centers of the Fertile Crescent.

The vision shook me to the core of my being. We are not in control. We are guests on the planet, guests in life. On the things that truly matter, we are basically powerless. For the first time in my life, I could see as I looked toward the stars that I was a creature, that I was someone who had in some fashion been created, and that neither I nor any other human creature could presume to be in control.

On that night of the Day of the Dead, an assumption which I never knew was a part of me was erased forever, the way the noonday sun erases the power of a candle. My faith in the competence and dominance of humankind was called into question. Once I had begun to doubt God. Now I had begun to doubt man.

I was in dismay, my confidence in humanity shattered.

What I did not know was that beyond those stars which were burning at me so brightly and inimically, the angels were practicing for a symphony of praise which would many months later burst on my behalf into the universe.

Lessons in Creaturehood

The rest of our time in Manaus flew by. Almost daily, extraordinary things happened to me, as if the Master Teacher had appointed angels to put a dull-minded pupil through exercises about life and destiny which followed up on the lessons which had been administered to me on the Day of the Dead.

One evening at dusk, as I walked from my class at the university down a street in a poor neighborhood, I saw a crowd of people gathered in front of a house, whose front windows and door opened directly onto the sidewalk. A small van pulled up in front of me and came to a halt at the curb. Two women stood in the light of the doorway, watching, dabbing at their eyes with white handkerchiefs. Some men in the crowd went to the tailgate of the vehicle and opened up the back. They took out the corpse of a middle-aged man dressed in a business suit with a tie. Directed by several old women who were gesturing and giving orders quietly, the men carried the body into the house. Through the paneless windows I could see them pass with their load through the living room and into a bedroom. They placed the man on the bed. The old women hurried the bearers out and closed the door. In the living room, the two women were seated on a couch, weeping softly. Those of us in the darkening street could watch everything going on inside the lighted house, as if it were a stage setting.

I went up to someone in the little group lingering around the doorway and asked what was going on.

Teve um enfarte hoje à tarde no centro. Morreu. "He had a heart attack downtown this afternoon. Just dropped dead."

I later learned that in Brazil, embalming is not the usual custom. Once the coroner is satisfied that a death is natural, the body is turned over to the family. In this case a friend who had a van simply brought the deceased to the house after the quick autopsy. The old women in the neighborhood were going to prepare the body for a wake that night and burial the next day—that was one of the functions old women exercised in Manaus. Carpenters were making a coffin from planks on which they would glue purple cloth, the mourning color of Brazil. The next day a school bus hired by the funeral arrangers would come to the home and take family and friends to the cemetery. The coffin would ride in the aisle of the bus.

On another occasion I was asked by the Baptists if I would be willing to do some tutoring in English for a group of high school students in a poor neighborhood on the outskirts of the city. I agreed.

Twenty-five eager students awaited me when I entered the classroom which was normally used for Sunday School. They were fascinated by the chance to practice their rudimentary English with a real American. As my tutoring session with these bright, lively kids unfolded, I learned that I was in a section of town where "second families" lived. Many Brazilian men had girl friends who, when they got pregnant, were installed in houses in this neighborhood. The men would visit their lovers when they could get away from their "first families," and some of the women were raising several children. The men paid the rent and living expenses sporadically for these second families until they got tired of the women or arranged for new partners or the "first wives" created an uproar.

Most of the mothers of my students wound up on their own sooner or later, and the Baptists were focusing on the children. They wanted to help them to educate themselves and get better jobs so that they could move out of the neighborhood, where there was a great deal of prostitution, crime and drugs. I went back to my own family that night remembering the faces of healthy, vigorous youngsters who were apparently facing their future bravely, but who were probably destined for lives of the deepest poverty. The boys would become unskilled laborers at minimum wage, and the girls would likely become mothers of the next generation of second families. It was all very discouraging.

Days later my attention was commanded by an event of a very different sort. Newspaper headlines began to scream about a massacre by Indians in the rain forest 150 miles from Manaus. A group of priests, nuns and handlers had been sent into the jungle to make contact with a tribe whose villages were set up in the path of the Trans-Amazonian highway, which in future years would link Manaus with the rest of Brazil. The expedition's purpose was to convince the Indians to move away from the road because such tribal groups almost always suffered disastrous consequences from contact with whites, either in the form of disease or destruction of their native culture. The missionaries had all been slaughtered. Military helicopters went into the jungle and brought back the remains. Our family went down to the square in the center of Manaus when the soldiers were lining up the little black boxes of bones for the press to photograph and film. I was surprised at how tiny the boxes were. The massacre had occurred only two weeks before, but insects and animals in the jungle had left only a few bones from most of the individuals.

There was only one survivor, the guide. It turned out that he was a Baptist. The American missionaries invited me to hear him give his testimony at a church the next Sunday night. His story was remarkable. He was a tall, skinny man, obviously unschooled, but he had known the jungle all his life and could speak the language of the tribe which the Catholic group had been commissioned to locate. He helped the group set up a base camp in the region where the nomadic Indians moved about in mobile villages. Through the guide, contact was made, and Indian leaders actually visited the base camp several times to talk with the head priest. Gifts were distributed, and everything seemed to be going well. Unfortunately, one of the Indian leaders stole a pistol during one of the visits, and the priest confronted the thief and forced him in public to return the weapon.

The guide had not been present during the encounter—he had been down at the river, a couple of miles away, doing some work on the boats which had brought the expedition from Manaus. He was exceedingly alarmed when the priest told him what had happened. He told the group that they were in great danger. The Indians had been humiliated. The chiefs probably would call the villages together and return with a war party to save their honor by slaughtering the whites. Only blood could wash away such shame.

"We have got to get out of here, now! If we don't leave today they will kill us!" the guide urged.

The priest refused to believe him. As head of the expedition, he was not going to jeopardize the mission because of a matter of petty theft. The guide pleaded. The priest was unmoved. During the night, the guide could hear the Indians signaling to one another. He grew terrified. Attack was imminent. When he could not persuade the priest to leave the next morning, he knew that all of them would die. He told the priest that he at least was getting out of there. The priest contemptuously dismissed him, and the agitated guide rushed out of the base camp and ran to the river where their boats were moored. He was distraught. Desperate with guilt, he returned to the base camp to make one more attempt to convince the group of the danger.

He found the priest in his path, dead, a six-foot arrow sticking out of his back. He had been trying to flee toward the river when they brought him down. A hacked nun lay nearby. The guide could hear the attackers shouting in triumph further along the path toward the base camp. He turned and raced back toward the river. The attackers heard him and were quickly on his trail. He left the path and made his way through the thick undergrowth, eventually reaching the riverbank downstream from the boats, which the Indians were busy pillaging. Warriors were all around him in the jungle. His only hope was the river. Miraculously, he saw some tree trunks floating near the shore where he stood in panic as warriors approached. He plunged in, swimming under water until he could come up between two of the logs. He linked the tree limbs together with his belt, and slowly began to drift down the river, his head above water, but hidden from the view of anyone on shore or even in a canoe on the river, unless the canoe came very close.

For two days and nights he floated with the current. He could hear the Indians along the banks, searching for him. The third day, all sound of the warriors ceased. On the fourth day, at night, he dragged himself to shore, shriveled and water-logged.

He could hear the military search copters but was afraid to try to attract their attention because the warriors might get to him before the army did. A week after the massacre, he heard voices around a campfire in the night. They were speaking Portuguese. It was a party of jaguar hunters from near Manaus. They gave him food and took him back to the city.

Newspapers at first blamed the guide for deserting the expedition. The military, more savvy about the ways of the Indians, knew that the guide had probably done all that he could do. The priest had in his zeal committed a deadly blunder by not listening to an experienced guide.

As the tall man spoke in the church that Sunday evening, I could see that he was not used to talking before groups. He did his narrative simply, with no embellishment. He was a storyteller, not a theologian. His eyes were still haunted as he remembered and recounted the details of his ordeal. His gratitude, and that of his wife, who sat near him as he stood uneasily before the pews filled with people, was profound. He did not know why all those good people in the Catholic expedition had died while he survived. He only knew that God had been good to him. His escape was a miracle. He knew that the Indians should have found him. He communicated his thanks to "*O Senhor*" with a simplicity and genuineness that I had never before encountered in a church.

There were many other experiences in which life and love and death in the Amazon were apportioned into my mind in ways which slowly brought home to me the possibility there might be deeper meanings in life, deeper voices, than my philosophy had allowed for. At the time the experiences all seemed separate and distinct, unlinked to one another. As time went on and I looked back on them, they took on a strange coherence. It was as if an invisible author or master of plots was weaving patterns into my life at the deepest subliminal level, preparing me for something which was to come.

The Quest

In early December, my family flew back to the U.S. I stayed behind alone because someone at my university wheedled a somewhat unwilling U.S. State Department into providing a small grant so that I could visit Rio and Brasilia and get to know more about Brazil than the Amazon could offer. I was to join my family back in the States in time for Christmas.

But my adventures were not over. As I traveled alone, there were more marvelous sights and happenings which I took for granted at the time, but which I later came to see as further exercises derived from the lessons administered to me on the Day of the Dead just a few weeks earlier.

Days before I was to leave the country, a major revolution took place in the Brazilian government. Authorities in Amazonas got quite nervous about an American professor who, in their eyes, had connections with the State Department and thus might be left-wing or a spy for the CIA. A customs officer at the Manaus airport stopped me as I was preparing to board the plane for home. The passengers on the big jet waiting on the tarmac sweltered in Amazonian heat as the official pondered whether my departure would be a threat to the new revolution. I realized that I might be taken to a military jail and put through an interrogation that I did not even want to think about. My Brazilian friends took the man aside and argued with him. For almost an hour it was touch and go. All of a sudden the official slapped my passport and papers down on the counter in front of the nervous airline employees, and waved me toward the jet. "You can go!" he said, as if in exasperation. To this day, I don't know why that customs official changed his mind so quickly and allowed me to leave. My own persuasion had obviously had no effect. I wondered later if some of my Brazilian friends had slipped him a bribe. At any rate, I finally was allowed on board, to the relief of the plane full of unhappy passengers. The unnerving experience was a parting shot from the Amazon to me, a final, quite firm reminder about the many forces beyond my control which swirled about me and affected my life. I returned with relief to my familiar world in the United States.

Except that world was no longer as familiar as it once had been. It was radically different. Better said, I was different. I saw my world with altered, less sure eyes.

You would think that someone whose whole view of life had been rocked by the realization that he was a creature would have moved directly into some kind of relationship with the One who had created him. Creature implies creator, does it not? I am afraid things were not so simple with me. I might have been a creature, but I was still an atheistic creature. The layers of my godless faith might have been peeled away one by one, but I still had no convincement that there was a God. I was just no longer certain that there wasn't one.

I must have amused the angels mightily. I threw myself into a quest for God, setting out to find Him, if indeed He existed.

I did everything wrong. I conducted my quest for God in the same way I conducted my class preparation and research projects as an academic. I got together bibliographies on God. I read piles of books and articles. I took notes. I kept a journal. I discussed my unbelief with Christian apologists, hoping they could convince me. I visited churches, everything from Unitarian to Calvinistic in order to give every shade of opinion a fair hearing. I went to hear itinerant evangelists , I went to small house churches where I was freaked by messages in tongues, with accompanying interpretation.

Everything that could be done (by my lights), I did. I was exceedingly active and preposterously open-minded. I wound up with a list of specs for what God would have to be if I were going to believe in Him. Moreover, I am afraid my attitude was, "When God gets me, He's going to know He's got a real prize." I was blissfully unaware of my pride. But if ever anyone could have worked his way to God, could have discovered Him through the exercise of intelligence and imagination and hard work, I would have done so. Had I not been told that scripture said, "Seek, and ye shall find?" So I sought. Diligently.

But I neither believed nor had faith. However much I quested, I still could not make myself believe that God existed and cared what happened to me.

"Hey, come watch the professor," the angels must have chortled. For a year and a half after I returned from the jungle, I must have been comedy central for many of them. I chased after God frantically. I knocked on every door I could find to pound. But God for me remained an abstract—a potential, not a reality. And my heart remained empty, and I ached, I did not know for what.

It may be that angels don't just laugh. Maybe they also weep.

The God Who Comes

I doubt that anyone who has ever known that they were far from God can ever forget the moment that they first came to know Him.

During all these months, I heard a great deal of religious talk. As I said, I had my own notions about who God would be when I finally favored Him with my belief. I knew lots of Pentecostals and Charismatics. I saw some of them receive what they called the baptism of the Holy Spirit. They would pray for the Spirit to infill them, usually in a circle of others who prayed with them, sometimes loudly. Often nothing happened. But on occasions I would see a person's face suddenly change. Surprise would come over them, and it was as if they were suddenly electrified with happiness. They would often begin to cry out in joy, and continue to do so sometimes for hours. It was a beautiful thing to see.

On the other hand, I frequently heard stories about people who were knocked to the floor in a faint and had to be revived, or bawled in grief and soggy repentance for hours on end. I was frightened of such a possibility. When I read the story in the Book of Acts of the Apostle Paul's being thrown into the dust by a shattering light as he approached Damascus, I figured that something similarly nasty—clean, clinical and lacerating — would be administered to me. My coming to God, I was certain, would be a very painful experience. I too would be thrown into the dust. I would be thoroughly humiliated, as I felt I deserved. I would babble and froth at the mouth, shaming myself in the eyes of anyone who happened to be an onlooker.

I wound up in a strange state of expectancy. I felt that I was on the verge of discovering God. I could almost see Him, except for some unaccountable shutter closing out His light. It was as if He was there directly in front of me, separated from me only by something like a tissue no thicker than transparent plastic wrap, but a film which marked the frontier between uncrossable dimensions of reality. I imagined touching that tissue with my palms and finger tips, and feeling palms and finger tips on the other side. His face seemed ten-thousandths of a centimeter from mine, yet I couldn't see it! So close, yet infinitely removed from me by the mysterious barrier! How could I bridge it? How could I penetrate it?

Eventually, I came to the end of my tether. I felt that God had done something in the Amazon, but I wasn't absolutely sure God existed. I could be fooling myself. I had worked so hard, I had striven so much for belief. And I was empty. As prepared as I was for faith, I was no nearer belief in God than I had been all during the twenty years of my atheism. I had hope that there was a God, but that was all.

I assumed despairingly that was the way I would spend the rest of my life.

One spring night, almost two years after I sat on the roof of the cabin cruiser in that cove in the Amazon River, I arranged to meet three friends at their house near the university. I went without food for forty-eight hours before our meeting, an enormously long fast for someone who had never done a spiritual fast and knew nothing about how to do it properly. One of the friends brought out a loaf of flat bread he had made, and a jar of honey.

"We will celebrate after we pray," he smiled.

They prayed for God to reveal His Spirit to me. I felt so awkward, so on the spot. They prayed for an hour, then still another. Nothing took place. Absolutely nothing. I was in neutral.

I tried to do my part, to concentrate, to place my attention on God, wherever He might be. "Is my prayer," I wondered, "nothing but bouncing thoughts off the inside of my skull? Does my pleading actually go anywhere outside me? Is there Anyone to hear?" I wanted the prayers answered, but at the same time I dreaded receiving the reply which I was sure would bowl me over and grind me to a pulp, if ever I came to know God.

I have learned in the three decades since that night that the sense of God's presence almost always arrives accompanied by surprise, dollops of surprise. Moses went to investigate a burning bush and found Glory. Elijah expected wind, earthquake and fire, and was stunned by a still, small voice. John the Baptist could scarcely credit that he had found the Messiah in a mere slip of a man from Galilee.

The surprise for me was that I never actually found God. He found me instead. The initiative turned out to be from Him, not from me.

I was in the midst of friends a few blocks from the university where I worked, but suddenly it was as if I were back in the tropics, on top of that boat where I had for the first time received an impression that I had been brought into being by Something beyond myself. That sense of being a creature descended upon me again, but this time in front of my amazed eyes I saw, instead of truculent stars and cold dark space, a shifting ocean of glowing light and soft shadow, a sea of life which stretched out infinitely before me. As if I were by myself on a quiet beach, I was gazing at waves tumbling toward me like gentle surf. Lovely, caressing whitecaps of moon-glow billowed upon me, splashing over my skin and enveloping my body until I was immersed in captivating light. My heart beat with quiet, steady joy at the deliciousness of this surprising baptism. An indescribable sense of both power and tenderness flooded my mind.

It was not that the light was God. Not for an instant did I have such a blasphemous impression. Rather, without being God, the light seemed to come from His unseen presence and expressed the radiant manner in which the LORD rationed to my finite mind and tiny spirit, without bursting them, the sweet sense of His Being, of how alive and beautiful and infinitely tender He was. The light was not itself the LORD, but it allowed me to know Something ineffable and exalting that I had never known before.

I could not tell anyone how long this bathing in billows of moonlight lasted. I don't think it was for very long. I doubt that I gave much sign of what was happening, but somehow my friends knew. Perhaps they could feel my exultation. Overawed, I said very little. They had been kneeling. Now they sat back silently.

We ate the bread, lacing it with honey.

As I drove home alone in the car, a voice within me taunted, "Tomorrow, you will doubt this. You will ask yourself, 'Did anything really happen?'"

I was unperturbed. I had spent my adult life in doubt about God. The doubt, I now assumed, had been given to me by the LORD, and He might give it back to me again. If so, I could trust Him. He would be in the doubt as He had been in the light. It was an utterly reassuring thought. Nothing would ever happen to me that He was not involved in! What astonishing comfort that living light had left behind!

No, this night was no mistake or illusion. I knew the LORD, not because in desperation I had concocted a startling experience. God had indeed come to me. His Spirit had flowed into mine. I knew that I would never be the same again in any way, even as a doubter.

And so it has proved for three decades. My sense of His unceasing Presence with me has deepened and grown more varied with the passing of the years. He has spent the thirty years since those two nights, one on a tropical river and the other in my own hometown, shaping the resistant material of my heart into the form of His own heart. He does this shaping with all His children. It continually amazes me that once He comes to them, the very beat of His children's hearts keeps time with the throb of their Creator's heart. Second advents are not a necessity.

Obviously, God deals with each of us in different ways. In my case, He has never ceased to transform me slowly and quietly, as gently as when He visited my spirit in that luminous surf. Others perhaps He does bowl over and grind to a pulp, if that is what they need. Like a good father, like a friend or bridegroom, He personalizes everything for us, tailors all His self revelations to fit the heart that He is attaching.

My story, as I look back on it, does not really seem to be my story at all. My life and its adventures and themes appear to be God's story, a narrative He authored and knit together, making of my existence a marvelous piece of art, with surprising spiritual resonances which were far beyond my unaided capacity to conceive and bring about.

Since I am a professor, I have of course been obliged to draw lessons from all the wondrous things that have happened to me, and I trust you will indulge my academic habit. I have the impression of being given constant pop quizzes and an occasional mid-term exam on what God is teaching me.

I myself express the lessons I have learned in several ways. For one thing, we human beings chase God, but when the hunt is up, we discover that all along, we ourselves have been the prize. I thought I had spent my life knocking on the door of Glory for entry, but when the door opened, I discovered that it was actually hinged inward, toward me, and that the rapping I considered mine was actually His. In a way we can hardly take in, He comes to sup with us, not we with Him.

And the angels? I do not want to add to the foolish nonsense that is being purveyed about them today, but signs of their activity are every-where, if we will but look and listen. Just as God on occasion beams Holy light on our retinas so that we can begin to know what it is like to dwell with Him, so God constantly dispatches angels to tinker with everything that happens with us. The angels not only refashion the events of our lives. They collect and string them into grand stories set in the brilliant light of eternity, showing us, if we will but see, that no occurrence in our time under the sun is ever insignificant, no act ever trivial.

The angels sent to me appear to have been gifted with a special penchant for humor. They have brought comic relief to those corners I have so busily painted myself into. I, who saw my existence as confined to atoms and molecules, as constricted within the time and space continuum of perishable material reality, now glory each day in the limitless destiny to which I am truly called.

It is the soft laughter of the angels, which I sometimes catch even when most surrounded by darkness, that comforts me that I am ever on the path of bright promise which God has prepared for all His children.

AFTERMATH:
The Fellowship
of Story

"But what happened after that night?" a new agnostic friend recently interrogated me after he had heard one or two bits of my story.

Thomas Cameron was a British academic, deeply imbued with the agnostic faith of his nation and the American university environment which he had chosen as the place to spend his life. He was visiting our campus and had asked me what research project I was working on.

What I was working on was the book which you now hold in your hand. Since such material on the dreams and idiom of God was not recognized as the kind of research that professors conventionally carried out, I was reluctant to talk about it. I had been deliberately evasive with Thomas.

"I am working on mini-biographies," I told him imprecisely, and attempted to change the subject.

Thomas, however, had been persistent, and I found myself telling him in sketch form the story of that fishing expedition on the Amazon and—as he pressed me with questions—the extraordinary blessing of light which had been given me. In the sketchiest terms, I brought up glory and grace. He was fascinated.

As I had thought would be the case, however, when he heard that I had become a Christian, he was aghast.

"Christianity!" Thomas's tone was one of shock. Despite his inbred civility, his lips were twisted in scorn.

"I have had one or two numinous experiences in my life too," Thomas averred, "and if I had gone through what you describe, I would probably have set up as a Shaman or Guru. But Christianity! I cannot understand how you were drawn to Christianity, of all things."

Thomas was genuinely baffled. How could any responsible academic be so out of touch?

Thomas's research specialty was the conquest of Mexico. He knew a great deal about how pious Catholic conquistadors had marched into the New World with their superior weaponry, their alphabet, and their obsessions, sacking the templed cities they found in their path, causing the death of millions of native people through siege and disease, and ruthlessly subjecting the survivors to vassalage and slavery. All the while they had carried the cross in their processions; they had allowed it to dangle from their necks as they had raped female captives. And they cloaked their depredations in the ideology of the Catholic Kings and the Renaissance Inquisition.

For Thomas, Christianity and rapacious doubletalk were synonymous.

I was tempted to offer an explanation to my new colleague, but limited myself to an inner sigh. We were in an airport lounge waiting for the departure of his plane. I did not try, in twenty minutes, to talk about matters which across decades had come to grip my heart, such as the Dream of God and the magnificence of Christ's Gospel Way of seeing reality. I also did not accede to his request to provide him samples of my writing. I could tell that he had caught a spark of the eloquence of the Gospel, but that glimmer within him was so blinkered by great learning and cultural sophistication that a few words or writings from me would not chase the shadows from his mind.

As is often the case, it was not the right time or place to talk of the Gospel.

I shook Thomas's hand firmly as I separated from him. I liked him immensely, but he and I could go no further on this occasion.

"Perhaps we'll be in touch again some day," I said vaguely in parting.

I was certain that Thomas, half warily, had expected that I would try to evangelize him. Wasn't that what Christians, with their deficient sense of diversity, did? He seemed intrigued, perhaps disappointed, that I chose the option of not doing so. Had he hoped that I would pull a rabbit out of the hat, would have something counterbalancing to offer about a faith which as a boy he had cherished, but which had long since been discredited in his eyes and in the milieu where he had chosen to dwell?

The Dream of God? And the Gospel as the final, powerful flourish of the Lord's sublime mode of creation and composition?

Thomas had heard very little of the story of the quest which you have just read, but I surmised that what made him catch his breath was the Gospel notion that God had discovered me, not vice versa, that one of the Lord's great attributes is that He comes to us, not that we labor our way to Him through intellect or insider spiritual practices. Had Thomas heard a reasoned argument claiming this attribute for the relation of God and human beings, he with his quick, confident intellect would have dispatched the claim with relish and gone on his Oxfordian way. But the brief word sketch he had wormed out of me of a night on the Amazon River and surf-light in a hippie cottage off Lake Avenue had caught his fancy. He knew that slicing up logically what I had told him would have been like fighting flames with a dagger.

Thomas would have been even more scornful if he had known the approach I had taken once awareness of God's reality was firmly implanted in my mind by the light. I had never in my quest had any interest in merely believing in deity, in some kind of impersonal Force or Providence or the All or the Ineffable, any more than I was interested in believing in Zeus, Osiris or Huitzilopochtli, or worshiping the sun or the moon. I had set my course clearly as a seeker: I aspired to adore the God Whom Abraham and Isaac worshiped, Whom the psalmists and Isaiah exalted, and Who Jesus told His disciples was their Father. Nothing else would suffice for me.

I took for granted that the light which was cascaded upon me that evening when my Knoxville friends prayed for me was not divine Essence but was rather a personal Appeal—an appeal from a Person—, calling me into fellowship with Someone Who was beyond my capacities of imagining or conceiving, but Who had revealed all that I needed to know on first acquaintance about His Person in the ancient texts of the Bible and in the body formed by His church.

I was seeking the face of YHVH-ADONAI, exemplified in the countenance of Christ Jesus! None other!

To do so after that night of glorious moon surf, I entered the world of evangelical Christianity, a world that would have excited Thomas's scorn. Every Sunday morning I went to church for two to three hours of service. Every Sunday evening, I went to church again, this time for two hours of worship and testimony. Every Wednesday evening, I met with a small group of other believers for prayer and study of the Bible. Every week, I had breakfast or lunch or a coffee break with friends during which we discussed Christian writing together or talked about what was going on in our experience of the Gospel. We prayed for one another constantly. I studied and memorized and taught. I served on church boards and with para-church organizations. I went with believers on weekend retreats for worship and self-examination.

This had been my pattern for thirty years, a not uncommon one for those of us in the evangelical subculture. How contemptible my world would have seemed to Thomas had I been unwise enough to try to communicate its nature to him in a conversation or a few samples of my writing!

But what an absorbing, exciting world it appeared to me as I looked back on it! My life in the Christian counterculture had been filled with more variety and diversity than I had encountered even in the university, and more adventure and creativity than I had enjoyed through philosophy, literature and scholarship. It had offered me greater stimulation than I had found in all the libraries, theaters and galleries I had visited in North America, Europe and South America!

Yet as different as I had made the course of my life from that which Thomas was leading, I would have agreed with him on one point: all the church-going, all the sermons and study and work and fellowship in Christian circles were not enough. Such activities prepared the terrain of my soul in an essential way, but they would have remained as sterile as Thomas perceived them without God's sowing His reality with grand eloquence into my mind and heart.

The Wednesday evening before I met Thomas, a suggestive event had taken place at my church, Bethesda Christian Fellowship. About twenty people were attending, and the Pastor, Morris Bagwell, asked each of us to tell about a sermon we had heard years before which had had such a great impact on our life that we were still influenced by it. My wife Mary B. told about a sermon by Tom Griffiths, a pastor at the Mumbles Baptist Church in Swansea, Wales, who did a sermon built around the refrain, "How dare you grumble in the presence of the Lord?"

"Even today, several years later, whenever I find myself wanting to whine about some difficulty in my life," Mary B. told us, "I recall that refrain: 'How dare you grumble in the presence of the Lord?'"

Allie Williams cited a sermon that Paul Cowell did several weeks after his son Brian was killed by a replica of a Kentucky long rifle in a freak hunting accident. Paul told the congregation that Brian's death had showed him something he had never known about the vastness of God's love. Paul looked directly at the members of his congregation, many of whom had been good friends for many years.

"Brian's death was the worst pain I have ever faced," he told them. "It was agony. As much as I love you, my friends, there is not a one of you here that I would give up my son's life to save. I would be willing to die myself to save you. But I would not give up Brian for you. But God did exactly what I could not do. He loved you so much that He gave up His son so that you could live more abundantly."

Pastor Morris went around the room, and most of those attending gave an example of a sermon which had affected them. I was sitting on my pew beside Mary B. in a bit of a panic.

I could not think of one single sermon I had ever heard. All I could remember was stories from sermons, not the sermons themselves.

When my turn came, I told of Pastor Ken Miles when he was a young man. His church could not yet pay him enough to live on, so he drove a school bus for extra cash. One day he was alone in the big yellow bus and began to make up songs of praise to the Lord as he wound his way to his garage. Ken, unfortunately, had a terrible singing voice. He was a growler with only one harsh note. He imagined the angels around the throne of God holding their ears and wincing as his pitiful melody floated upward.

"That guy can't carry a tune in a bucket," they complained to one another. "He's awful!"

The Lord, in Ken's fantasy, waved the angels quiet. "Hush! I want to listen to Ken Miles's song for me. I like it! Bach never pleased me more."

I could recall stories, but not a single sermon. I could not even identify for sure the point that Ken had made with his story.

Sermons were not my only weakness as a religious learner. I also had trouble memorizing scripture, a feat most evangelicals take for granted. I simply could not retain the commonest scripture for any great length of time.

But stories! Stories went into my mind and combined with other stories, forming swirls and clusters from which meanings irradiated that I could not arrive at otherwise. Fellowship with Christ for me was conducted by means of dialogue and plot, character and scene, and very little by abstraction or citation.

The Dream of YHVH-ADONAI and the eloquence of Christ's Gospel! Who can express what it is like to have heard and absorbed them? New Testament scripture says in the Book of Mark that Jesus never taught the public without story. In private He hammered wondrous truths at the disciples who were close to Him, but to the masses who were curious or merely desperate He responded with parables. And Christ's narrative method was successful! The minds His parables cultivated for the Gospel would in time combust into the vigor of the early church. But first He allowed the magic of story to work its slow way into the psyche of His hearers. Sometimes His parables were recounted in His own voice, at other times expressed in the extraordinary things He enacted.

Thomas Cameron had experienced through contact with my story the parable effect, the beckoning toward truth which distinguished Jesus's public ministry.

As I unlocked my car after leaving the airport lounge, I was marveling that I was myself a good example of Christ's seeding with parable. I had as a student and professor encrusted myself in the carapace of what Isaiah called "seeing without seeing and hearing without hearing." It was as if I had been a 20th century member of the crowds which had peopled the leaves of the Book of Mark, somewhat attracted to Jesus of Nazareth, but deep down firmly attached to my own culture, my own immortality projects and substitute gods, and reluctant to shed them for the untried splendors Christ claimed to offer.

So the Lord persistently used story—scene, event, episode and character —to change my modes of perception and habits of thought, to draw me toward His ways, just as He had done with people 2000 years before in Galilee and Jerusalem. The events in the Amazon accumulated in effect and combined with other events that I scarcely noticed until over two years after I returned to the States I was ready to be baptized in ineffable moon surf. Story had brought me to that night and its visitation of light.

And more story had been used to carry me beyond it.

Stories, always stories, were employed by Christ to draw me to Him and equip me for the further stories He had in mind. Divinely elaborated scene, event, episode, atmosphere and character had shattered my atheism, had persuaded me that life was not fixed in the unalterable molds of death and evil which the world took for granted, but in God's hands was to be transformed beyond anything we now knew or could imagine.

How perfect! The Gospel quintessentially drew and schooled those it blessed through the humble medium of narrative! And how marvelous for me to learn at long last that stories were the elements through which the Lord prepared a mediocre person like myself for the sunburst of the Gospel.

Twelve years before, my brilliant pastor friend Paul Cowell had asked me if I would help him ground his new congregation in the history of Christianity. Paul had observed during his years as a pastor that Christians were familiar with precious little of their rich heritage. He asked me to present the story of some great hero of the Christian faith briefly during each morning service. Paul saw story as an integral part of worship.

I began composing oral biographies, each from ten to thirteen minutes in length. Across the years I delivered between two and three hundred of them to our congregation. From Biblical figures through the early church martyrs like Perpetua, and then Augustine of Hippo and Patrick of Ireland, Francis of Assisi, Thomas à Kempis, John Woolman, Charles Haddon Spurgeon, Dwight L. Moody, Fanny Crosby, Ruth and Billy Graham, C.S. Lewis, Mother Teresa and hundreds of others, I related incidents from their lives before our congregation.

At some time during those years, an unexpected awareness arose in me that the lives and stories of these splendid people had been put together by a hidden hand, that I was merely narrating lives which had been plotted and articulated by a creative mind immeasurably grander than mine or that of my subjects. I saw how random event fitted into random event, coincidence into coincidence, in what turned out to be the most unrandom and uncoincidental way. Uncovering hidden design became my greatest delight and challenge as a narrator and spiritual biographer.

What especially surprised me was that some of the most powerful intimations of divine narrative came to me as I related the lives not of the spiritual giants that I found in the annals of Christianity, but in the stories of commonplace, everyday people whom I knew personally. After years of studying accounts of famous Christians, I gradually began to shift my focus to narratives that I pieced together not from conventional research, but from contacts within my own circle. I never had to seek such stories deliberately. They flowed in. It was as if I were a magnet, drawing amazing tales and yarns into my rapidly multiplying stock from the everyday encounters of my life.

I came to regard myself as something like the host of a little crossroads inn through which extraordinary people passed and rested for a time to spin me their tale before they went on their way: Lowell and Preacher Gordon, Coy and Betty Sue, Sophie, Garlan and Helen, Amanda and Abby.

I learned of love, death, villainy, old houses, the benevolence of uncles, the betrayal of spouses, triumph, failure, pathos, voyages, angels, strange coincidence—all the elements of fine story telling were dropped in my lap by my friends and acquaintances, or revealed from my own life. The accounts came so thick and fast that I could scarcely find time to tell them all, and yet I felt compelled to exercise my simple office as story-telling host of my own *Maison Dieu*, my pilgrim's inn, through which people on a quest for the sacred passed. I was obliged to invent nothing. My only task was to narrate what I was told or experienced. My humble function was to honor the stories and craft them into forms where they like sparks could ignite combustible already spread abroad by the Holy Spirit.

The word "Gospel" came to hold two crucial meanings for me. "Gospel" was in one sense a word for a particular kind of narrative collection, stories in which YHVH-ADONAI came unbidden into the lives of His children to help them reach their highest destiny. The books of Matthew, Mark, Luke and John were made up of tales of little people—Martha anxious in her kitchen, a Roman centurion too humble to bother the Master, Zaccheus in a sycamore tree—to whom YHVH-ADONAI through Christ demonstrated that they mattered supremely to Him as He passed by quickly, His very shadow changing their lives forever.

But the word Gospel also referred to the grand saga which ennobled human life with hope and courage and high ideal, the vast story of YHVH-ADONAI pursuing men and women in order to save them for eternity at the same time that He stalked Death and Evil so that He could destroy them forever in a stupendous finale to the history of the world as we knew it, a consummating cosmic act restoring reality to the track of its glorious first purposes.

All of the elements of the Gospel exercised their magic upon me, but it was these last components, the stalking of Death and Evil by Christ and the certainty that He would destroy them and lead a people that He was calling to an eternal Celebration of Victory and Peace, which came to have the deepest resonances in my soul. The picture of that Day at the end of history when Christ will fling death, Hades and Satan into the Lake of Fire seared itself into my brain and became the central image of life for me, the image which organized all other images around it.

What now humbles me most was how many years it took me, a supposedly intelligent and well informed man, to realize the true nature of the Gospel. Stoutly I resisted its truth, but ever so slowly I came to recognize that the Gospel was not a matter of propositions and laws, temples and rites and pieties. It was a way of seeing reality, of incorporating everything that we perceive within the frame of Christ's action against evil and mediocrity, and His coming victory over them. The Gospel was more like an informing culture within than an external religion, more like a dynamic principle presiding over the mind rather than something assented to on the basis of reason and experience, even though both reason and experience were involved in practicing the Gospel. The Gospel was not something I grasped. It grasped me, tightly, the way the eye grasps images so that the eye of the mind can see. Such was the nature of its mysterious power.

The Gospel dreamed me as much as I dreamed it!

As I commenced to discern in the very process of my narration the interaction between the grand story of the Gospel and the commonplace materials I was dealing with in each relation, I was humbled. How could I, with my modest talent, compose stories of mothers and babes, young lovers in darkened churches, foot soldiers in trenches, and demented Southern ladies in nursing homes, and tell them in such a way that the narrations possessed as their illuminating frame the age of colossal victory which Christ promises when He comes back to recreate the reality in which all human life has its being? Yet as I reread my accounts, I detected that such an incipient vision had unconsciously informed my narrative design all along as I struggled to develop in my stories the fullest meaning of what I was composing.

The breakthrough moment for me as a narrator began just over a decade ago on a Sunday afternoon when I was driving down a winding and lonely highway from Fall Creek Falls campground, where I had spent five days alone under the trees and stars after my father's death. I was scheduled to tell a story of some hero of the Christian faith to our congregation at Bethesda Christian Fellowship that night. I had planned to tell the love story of John Newton, the author of the hymn "Amazing Grace," and his wife Mary, but instead of practicing my presentation of their lives as I rode along in my car, I found myself weeping over the memory of my father. As I took the curves of that two-laned road across the Cumberland

Plateau, I was encountering the twists of my father's life in a way that I had never seen them before. He had ruined himself with alcohol and sexual extravagance. He had damaged his wife and children and those around him with his terrible inattentions. Yet that evening the story of his failed life recomposed itself within my mind so that the hand of God appeared, and when I told the love story of Garlan and Helen to my friends at Bethesda Christian Fellowship, many of them wept, not at the loss represented by my father's life, but at the beauties which grace had spun into its tapestry.

As time went by I told the tale of my father and his sad but remarkable life on other occasions. Sometimes I told it to my students as a listening exercise in Spanish or in Portuguese classes. I found that the young people were as moved by it as the Bethesda congregation had originally been, even though they heard it in a foreign language they knew imperfectly.

After pondering the effect of the tale on the most varied audiences, I went to my keyboard one morning and when at the end of the day I sat back from my completed text glowing brightly on the computer screen before me, I felt awe. Not at my story—it held all of my inadequacies as a writer—but at a strange certainty which was emerging in my mind from that day's process of composition, i.e., not only that the Lord had all along been configuring my father's life, but that I had been commissioned to narrate its mystery.

That sense of commission completed my breakthrough.

I put the title "Garlan and Helen" over the story. Writing the work intensified my awareness that the Lord had indeed arranged people, events, atmosphere and apparent happenstance in the life of my father and a lost love of his youth. This awareness grew stronger and more focused as other stories came my way, and the months and years went by. In every narrative I wrote, I encountered the generous action of YHVH-ADONAI and Christ's Gospel. The more I wrote, the more my creative excitement mounted. Although I was nothing more than a modestly gifted artisan, I had been given a great artistic motif. Christ's yearning to penetrate every atom of human existence and to draw all reality into His bright orbit could be discovered in the ordinary stories of everyday human beings! Almost all of us ignored Christ's action in our lives, I found. But it was there for us to see if we wished or dared.

To compose such accounts became my consuming passion. I wrote and wrote. Most accounts were given solely for my personal use and will remain forever in my notebooks, but several appeared suitable for broader exposure. Eventually I gathered them into the collections which you now hold in your hand.

"What happened after that night?" Thomas Cameron had questioned me.

What happened was that a man of letters and books was exposed to a whole new genre of sacred literature, stories crafted in our time by the same Hand which had plotted the sagas of Jacob and Moses and mingled chronicle and poetry into the vivid biography of David the King. A vision of the Gospel Genre unfolded within me and around me. Just as Luke dipped into his sources and mined his day-by-day experiences with the Apostle Paul to present the Good News of Christ Jesus as God's glorious intromission into history and koiné life, I was given the privilege, in an exceedingly modest way, of relating the continuance of the Gospel process.

Luke became my mentor. He dreamed like God! And, however imperfectly, so could I! And so can we all!

What happened after that night, I can now answer Thomas Cameron, was that I have responded to the privilege as best I could. I have no question whatsoever that other more gifted writers could have done it better. I hope they will do so in the future.

For me, to have carried out my commission is a reward beyond any that I could have imagined in those long years when I, like you, Thomas, was conducting my quest, those years before, as John Newton put it, I was found.

And in the stories to come, Thomas, I will relate to you some of the rewards which came to me, and come to all believers, when God opens up the lives of His children.

Here ends Part One of To Dream Like God, recounting the narrator's quest to find and know his Creator.

Part Two contains the stories which the narrator was enabled to tell once his mind was regenerated, starting with the Moonsurf of Light.

The

Eloquence of God

PART TWO

of

To Dream Like God

In Memory of J.O. Brock, barber.
He was
literally and spiritually
a Doorkeeper in the House of the LORD.

He was a good man, a quiet man,
The soul of generosity.
He became a model for me and many others,
but in his meekness,
he almost certainly did not know that he was doing so.

But God knew!

Introduction

The Eloquence of God! How incessantly He calls His children! How He uses the finest details of life as rhetoric to draw humankind toward Him!

In Part One of To Dream Like God *I recounted how I moved from atheism to the belief that God exists. To be perfectly frank, I assumed (naïvely) that I had arrived, that believing in the existence of God was the ultimate step I was to take. Consolidation and firming up of that belief was what I would do for the rest of my life—so I thought.*

I of course was not taking God Himself into account. Over the next several years, he was moving in my life, edging me past mere theism toward the Gospel, which, as you will see by the end of Part Four of To Dream Like God, *is several dimensions beyond passive acknowledgment that God exists. The Gospel calls us, beguiles us and impels us not only to transformation but to action.*

And the vehicle which God employed to change me in a Gospel way was story. He flooded my life with stories, one after another across many years, true stories that I was told or watched unfold. All taken together, they added up to a kind of eloquent language whose components were event, action, atmosphere, character, suspense and theme, and whose purpose was to instill within me the magic and holy chemistry of the Gospel, especially the atom-splitting promise of the Second Coming of Christ. It was as if God was using the stories of my life in the same way that Jesus had employed parables in His day, preparing those who heard Him for greater changes still to come.

The stories which introduced me to the concept of the Eloquence of God seemed to fall naturally into sets, which I called chronicles because of my love of the way so many medieval narrators saw, as I do, the unfolding of lives and kingdoms in their times through the lens of the Gospel.

*The first set of stories which exercised the parable effect on me I have grouped under the heading, **Chronicles of Zion Springs**. Many other pieces from the same family of stories and journal entries were granted me over a period of about a dozen years, but I have chosen to include here only three of them. All of the accounts of this type grew out of a small North Carolina country church which was the center of the community which nourished me as a child. I called the church and its people Zion Springs, a type of name common in the South and thus representative of the beloved region which has formed me and many other evangelicals into the shapes which God has been pleased to use in His special way.*

The first selection, "Garlan and Helen," holds a warm place in my heart as a storyteller because it was the first example of what I call the Gospel Genre ever given to me. "Prayer Requests" and "Up Home" continue the evocation of how God was always calling to me through everyday occurrences and people, and the great simplicities of my childhood.

*The second section which I call **Chronicles of the Appeal** is made up of stories whose unifying theme is the action of Christ in appealing to all of us in the splendid languages of sign and event which He has created to incarnate the Gospel. Each story represents a hopeless situation which can have no good issue, exactly the kind of human dead-end into which the Gospel above all other religious expressions can paint joy. Hopelessness and death are the fields in which the Gospel explodes like a rocket from the throne of God.*

The penning of the stories in these two collections enabled me across a decade to discover the eloquence of God, that divine rhetoric which persuades us toward the actions and promises of Christ. Through what at first appeared to me to be merely good tales quarried from family memories and the testimonies of friends, I found myself enthralled by a mysterious flow of power which pointed, like that night of surf-light (see "... And the Angels Laughed" in Part One), to something beyond itself.

Although these accounts do not reach the understanding of the Gospel which was in time to become the most significant blessing of my life, I honor them as worthy children of that evening when God favored me with my first glimpse of His Glory.

PART TWO

The Eloquence of God

⟨ caveat ⟩

Chronicles of Zion Springs

*(Three stories—flavored with the dreaming of God—centering on a
rural church in a North Carolina community)*

Garlan & Helen

Prayer Requests

Up Home

and

Chronicles of the Appeal

*(Three stories in which God appeals in manifold and sometimes
strange ways to His children)*

Apples & Bread & the Language of God

Philip

Mildred

Chronicles of Zion Springs
THE GOSPEL GENRE:
*God's Calling to the Narrator Across Time
and Through the Events
of His Everyday Life*

Garlan & Helen

This story of love, failure, and restored love begins in 1924 in the little town of Shelby, North Carolina. Garlan first told me he met Helen in the Blue Bird Ice Cream Parlor, but I now think Garlan's recollection may have been confused. Helen, whose memory seems reliable on this matter of where they first met, tells me that it was in a candy store beside the Carolina Theater.

"It was a cold winter day, and I came in to buy some sweets. I saw him standing in the back, warming his hands over a stove. He had on a long brown overcoat, and his hair was as black as coal and wavy. He was the most beautiful boy I had ever seen. I couldn't help myself. I stood there and stared."

Helen was 13. Garlan was 16.

Garlan and Helen were soon sneaking out together. Her parents did not want her dating at such a young age. He was the son of Preacher Gordon, a prominent Cleveland County Baptist pastor, and she was a blacksmith's daughter. Since Garlan had access to Zion Springs Baptist Church after hours, that's where he took Helen on their dates.

Within three months she knew she was pregnant. Both families reacted strongly. Preacher Gordon sent Garlan off to Bouies Creek Academy, in eastern North Carolina. Helen's family locked her in the attic for several weeks, to keep her away from Garlan. She would look out of the high window, hoping for glimpses of him. Eventually, her father and mother sold their home, gave up everything they had, and moved the family to Florida, so that they could all bear the shame away from the mocking eyes they imagined they saw on every side in Shelby, North Carolina.

The pregnancy was a hard one for the girl. A wisp of a child, tiny and skinny, she suffered from nausea and cramps. Her family never said a word of blame to her, but she was lonely and missed Garlan. At least in Florida her parents would let her get out of the house and go for walks down the dirt road passing the place they found to rent.

"I would get so tired and sick as I walked," she told me, *"that I would stop to rest at the house of some colored folks who lived at the end of the road. I'd just lie down on the porch with their dogs. Those people were so nice to me."*

She fell screaming to the floor of the bathroom on the day the labor pains began. Her family rushed her to the hospital. Helen's delivery was an agonizing one. The baby was normal sized, but Helen was so small, and the birth tore her body so badly that she would never have another child. She did not see the baby, a little boy. She was unconscious from her ordeal as they cleaned him and wrapped him, and took him away for adoption.

Garlan came back to Shelby from Bouies Creek Academy after a semester. To the best of my knowledge, he never tried hard to trace Helen. I think he had put her out of his mind. He was sixteen and heedless, and by now busy with other matters. He had lots of girl friends. He dropped out of school and worked here and there, selling Cokes and popcorn at the concession stand of the Carolina Theater or serving sodas behind the counter at the Blue Bird Ice Cream Parlor.

A few months after Helen's baby was born and taken away, she was out walking with her sister. On a nearby street, a lawyer lived, and on impulse one day, she dragged her sister with her and rang his doorbell. He must have been a kind man, looking down at those two thin faced, working-class girls on his porch.

"I don't want to make any trouble," she told him. *"I know I can't see the baby. But if I could just know he's all right, if maybe I could see his picture."*

Two weeks later, the lawyer saw her passing and motioned her in. He gave her a picture of a healthy baby boy clutching a toy. At Christmas time some years ago, Helen showed me that picture.

"*No,*" she answered me, "*I never learned what happened to him. He would have been of military age in the Second World War. If he survived it, he would be in his sixties now.*"

Back in Shelby, the years passed, and Garlan was restless and driven, as he would be all his life, moving from one job, one girl to another. On a trip to Alabama, he met Georgia, a petite brunette who was cashier at Bledsoe's Department Store in the little town of Thomasville. She was unhappy at home, and they eloped. Both were 19 years old.

The decades now fly by as these young lives take on the shape of middle age and beyond. The Great Depression comes, and then World War II. Garlan and Georgia have two sons. Garlan begins to drink and goes on binges every few months. Even though he was very intelligent and gifted with people, he would never rise in the world. Every time he moved up a rung of the ladder at the Jewel Tea Company or Standard Drugs or many other companies, he would fall back because he had disappeared on an alcoholic binge. And there were always other women.

Helen married also and settled in Miami. I don't know how happy her marriage was. I do know that Helen has never talked to me much about it. Since she and her husband could not have children, they adopted a little boy and raised him.

Her husband's death left Helen with very little money to live on. She went to the foster home service in Dade County, and offered to take care of children who needed a mother.

"*I did it, in a way, for the baby I gave up. I figured if somebody else had raised my baby, I wanted to try to return the favor to the Lord.*"

For twenty-five years Helen was a caretaker of handicapped children in her home. She specialized in the little ones nobody else wanted. One little girl—a thalidomide baby— was brought to her who had no legs and only one arm. She stayed with Helen until she was in her twenties. Another little girl was brain damaged and at the point of death when Helen received her. The child never learned to talk or walk or dress or feed herself. Almost the only thing this child could ever learn was to love Helen. She would slither across the floor and wrap herself around Helen's feet as Helen, lonely, talked on the phone in the evenings. Other suffering youngsters were brought to her with terrible convulsions or behavior problems. Helen had up to six of these children at a time living with her, while she also cared for her mother up until she died at the age of ninety. For two and a half decades, Helen lived taking care of people who could not take care of themselves, feeding, washing, tending the sick and infirm, with all of the tiredness and boredom and frustration and battles with filth and confine-ment of life that this involved.

"It was wonderful," she says. *"I loved every minute of it. I had such great kids. They helped out so much."*

Georgia and Garlan's life together began winding toward its conclusion. As age came on, Georgia became an alcoholic too, and although both she and Garlan were good workers, they lost their jobs because of their unreliability. I remember the Christmas when Georgia was so drunk she could not serve the dinner that she had prepared for us. But most of the time she was O.K., and as Garlan's health declined, Georgia took care of him, and did it stalwartly. They stopped drinking.

In 1979 Georgia suffered a massive stroke, and lingered between life and death for weeks. When she came out of it, she was an invalid, and her personality had changed. She was like a child. A gentle, beautiful spirit, but a child. I thought Garlan was lost, that he could not bear this blow. She had always been so strong, always there for him in his many infirmities, his lost jobs, his times in jail. I thought he would turn back to drink.

But Garlan became a caretaker. This man, who, deep down, probably did not know very well how to love, cared for Georgia selflessly, sacrificially, as if he was in some way trying to redeem all the suffering he had caused her. During the nine years he served her, I came to admire him as one of the most giving and noble men I had ever known.

Georgia died suddenly one night in 1988.

A friend of Helen's mailed her an obituary of Georgia's death. Helen waited an appropriate time and phoned. Her call began a long-distance courtship that lasted for months. I have seen the phone bills those two accumulated during that period. They must have chattered away like teenagers. Early on, they talked about getting together. Since her health was good, Helen proposed to take a Greyhound bus from Florida, but they kept postponing the trip for one reason or another. I believe it was because they were both afraid of seeing one another faded and withered, over sixty-five years since the last time they laid eyes on one another.

In June of 1989, she came. He met her at the Greyhound bus station, which now occupies the building which used to house the Carolina Theater, where he sold popcorn, and two doors down from the hole in the wall that used to be their candy store. For a week they gallivanted around Cleveland and Rutherford counties like delighted young lovers, visiting old places they held in common, dropping in on relatives Helen had lost touch with because she lived so far away.

"Should I marry her?" Garlan asked me.

"I don't think so," I responded. "Remember, it's been sixty-five years since you have seen one another. You have only been with her a week. You barely know her. And two eighty-year-olds can be just as miserable living together as two twenty-year-olds." I can't believe I mouthed to them the old cliché, "Marriage is a serious business at any age. Give it some time." I felt as if I were the aged one trying to talk sense into a couple of smitten youngsters.

The next thing I knew about the matter was that they had eloped. They went to Gaffney, South Carolina, where young couples in the mid-1920's used to sneak off to get married.

The months passed. Helen brought a new vitality to Garlan. When she came back into his life, he had been a rickety old man, fearful of his health, homebound, cautious of risks. She was impulsive. When she found he had not for years seen his last brother, who lived 500 miles away in Arkansas, she piled him into their old car and drove the distance in a day. He and his brother, who had thought they would never see one another again, clung to each other and laughed and wept, and Helen laughed and wept with them. On another occasion she drove Garlan on the spur of the moment to Florida—17 hours. Garlan, who had so drawn in from life, found his world renewed and brightened by Helen.

The marriage was not all smooth sailing. Garlan came to me and said they were quarreling, that she went hours and days barely talking to him. She would go into the little spare room in their trailer and sleep on the floor at night, away from him.

"I am afraid she is going to leave me," Garlan confided, as anxious as a young groom. Somehow, even though they knew as little about how to manage conflict in love as couples sixty years younger, they stuck it out. Helen stayed.

Six months after their marriage, I noticed that Garlan had virtually stopped talking when I visited him and Helen in the little beige trailer they were renting. His phone calls to me ceased. I attributed it to the depressions that had always afflicted him, but by early summer of 1990, it was becoming obvious that something more serious than melancholy was gnawing at him. In July, he was diagnosed as having two cancers, one in his liver and one in his lungs.

"He might live two months," the doctor told me.

And so Garlan set about the hard business of dying, and Helen of helping him to die. He rarely left his bed after July, and Helen attended him day and night. It was as if life had prepared her for this moment of helping her lover go into death. Helen has told me how they talked and wept in those last days together.

"What we did was so wrong," they sobbed to each other. *"But God brought us back together after 65 years. That is His sign that we are forgiven."*

Garlan lived several weeks longer than the doctor had predicted, mostly, I think, because of the exquisitely loving care that Helen bestowed upon him. As I visited them in the summer and on into the fall, I learned much of how holiness and love are connected as I watched this remarkable woman and this dying old man. I remember one midnight in that kitchen-living room of their trailer where a hospital bed had been installed by Hospice. Garlan had soiled the sheets badly. The smell in the room was disgusting. Helen handled it all with the tenderness of a mother and her baby, expertly heaving his body around, talking cheerfully all the time to him and to me, while I handed her towels. He looked like a refugee from Auschwitz concentration camp. He had lost fifty pounds, and his pallid skin was stretched over the bones of his face like wet paper. He was weak and exhausted by the ordeal of being cleaned up, but when it was over Helen impetuously gathered his skeletal face in her hands and kissed him firmly on the mouth. Juliet never kissed Romeo with greater love.

I am a religious man and have yearned all my life to know God. I have knelt before many altars seeking holiness. I never felt myself on more holy ground than I did that night when, amidst the stench of feces and the sight of a bucket of soiled towels, I watched Helen and Garlan, and I knew the love of God.

November the 18th, 1990, at four o'clock in the morning, my phone rang. "Yulan," my wife's voice said. "The Hospice nurse just called me. He's dead."

I crossed the mountains from Tennessee into North Carolina and drove up to Helen and Garlan's trailer. My wife met me at the door. "She cries like a child," my wife said. "Like a little girl. She has gone into the spare room and won't come out into the living room, because that's where he died."

Hospice workers had already moved the bed on which he lay for so many weeks. I looked at the empty space and then went into the little room where she was crumpled on a pile of blankets. Sobbing, she showed me a tattered brown overcoat. Garlan had saved that garment, she told me, down through the years.

I go to Garlan's grave as often as I can arrange to cross the mountains. He lies in the cemetery of Zion Springs Baptist Church, where his father was pastor and where, over sixty-five years ago, he carelessly brought his young lover, Helen. As I stand on the grass which has now grown over his grave, I remember the man who, like you and me, did not know how to love, but who had restored to him, by the goodness of God, an abundance of the graces of love.

Things come and go in life. The Blue Bird Ice Cream Parlor, the candy store, the Carolina Theater, Georgia, Garlan—they are all gone now. But love endures.

It is so hard for God to get His brush strokes into the portraits of our lives, but whatever our follies, however we mess up our lives fumbling for pleasure and ambition, and putting love off to the side of our agenda, God remains faithfully at work. He arranges ages and civilizations, individuals and events, bringing all things to full circle, so that the one eternal thing, love, always has the chance to emerge and endure.

If the angels in heaven have chronicles and tell one another stories, as we human beings do here, under the sun, I am sure that they tell the story over and over of the love of Garlan and Helen.

Prayer Requests

In English, the word "hero" does not refer just to those who are famous, whose great deeds influence masses of people. Personages like Plato, Charles Dickens, Winston Churchill, Eleanor Roosevelt, Mother Teresa, Billy Graham and Bill Clinton possess names which have been made famous by the world.

But the English language, in its wisdom, does not limit the use of the word "hero" to those who have achieved fame. English allows the word "hero" also to be used for the central figure of any drama or story. We talk about the "hero" of a play or novel. Oliver Twist is the hero of a famous novel. George Bailey is the hero of a film called "It's a Wonderful Life."

In this sense, all people, all of us, are called by our Lord to become heroes. You and I will never be famous in the world's eye, but we are heroes in God's dramas, with plots drafted in heaven itself. God is among us, working out His precious stories. His are all stories of love, of success and failure in love, here in time, under the sun.

He will honor His heroes in Eternity, when both time and the sun are no more.

I want to take you back earlier in our century for a tale of destinies.

The year is 1928. The scene is Zion Springs Baptist Church in Piedmont County, North Carolina. Zion Springs is a thriving country church with stately white columns and has a little bell tower beside the church porch. The building is situated on a green slope above two springs which give the church its name and provide pure and very cold water to anybody who wants to wander down after church.

The bell in the little tower, by the way, really works. It peals at 9:45 for Sunday School and sounds again to call everyone in for preaching. The men in the church, who usually wear bib overalls during the week, gather outside the building in starched white shirts and dark suits to smoke a cigarette before the bell calls them for the singing of hymns like "Victory in Jesus" and Preacher Gordon's forty minute sermon. Alongside Zion Springs, a graveyard filled with those gray, rounded family tombstones spreads out toward Bate Hamrick's pasture and barns.

The inside of the old church is unremarkable. There is a piano up front on the left as you face the pulpit, which is in the center, of course. Over in Charlotte at a Baptist church in the Providence Road section, they moved the pulpit off to the side, and when Bate Hamrick heard about it he showed his feelings by spitting his tobacco on a grasshopper twelve feet away and glowered worse than he did the time the Lattimore Cotton Gin truck ran over three of his coon dogs in the same day.

Up on the left front wall, beside the choir, there is one of those wooden plaques with hymn numbers on it for each service. A similar plaque beneath it announces the previous Sunday's offering. Wasps laze in and out the windows on hot Sunday mornings.

But I want to introduce you to certain members of the Hebron Youth Sunday School class, a group of youngsters who belong to farms around Zion Springs. Most of them were born between 1908 and 1915.

First, Myrtle Lee Crowder, a large girl who wears cotton print dresses all year round. She is a great big, graceless person, one of those that Southerners seeing her for the first time automatically call a gal. She's quiet and exquisitely shy. Her eyes will seldom meet yours. Her mother is Miss Dixie, one of the strongest willed women I have ever met in my life. She is the kind who would starch the daisies in the field beside her house if she could get around to it, but she is too busy running people's lives, especially Myrtle Lee's, who has always been a disappointment to her.

Myrtle Lee's cousin, Addie Green, is the exact opposite of Myrtle Lee. She is the most popular member of the group, pretty and skinny and vivacious and blonde, smart as a whip. She can talk your ear off and make you love it.

A gawky boy with glasses comes next in my introductions. His name is Hilary Bridges, and he is the lucky one Addie Green has singled out for her affection. Hilary is what a later generation will call a brain. He gets all A's at Lattimore High School, which the entire group attends, and where the Hebron Youth Sunday School teacher, Miss Edna, teaches. There are great hopes throughout Zion Springs that Hilary will go to Wake Forest College and make a preacher, and Addie Green would like very much to be a preacher's wife.

Next, I bring before you three youngsters named Megginson, two brothers and a sister. Buford is the oldest, the athletic looking one. He is tall and muscular, by far the best looking young man, some people say admiringly, in this end of the county. Good baseball player, can play every position, including pitcher, on Lattimore's team. Some people think he is a little too loud, a fraction too cocky. Miss Edna keeps telling him not to lord it over the others so much, but he's a natural born boss, maybe not really a leader, but he just likes to order people around. His sister Hessie is a delight of a person. She's willowy, has wavy brown hair, and a spirit as sweet and gentle as a dove. The youngest fellow in the family is Lowell, a delicate, sensitive boy with sandy hair and a spirit as mild as that of his sister Hessie. He is much overshadowed by his big brother, Buford, and in fact by about everybody else in the group except Myrtle Lee. He's shy and tentative, but unlike poor Myrtle Lee he's really quite likable because his eyes shine with friendship, and he seems to admire everybody he meets. The Megginson family lives over on Socrates Lee Road, near White Shoals Baptist Church, but they come to Zion Springs because Old Man Megginson, who loads cotton bales down at Dunlap Mills, got into a fight with the White Shoals pastor over the interpretation of Ephesians 4:23.

There are several others in the Sunday School class, but I'll mention just two more: Eudocia Hamrick is another cousin of Myrtle Lee. They call her Doshie. I think nowadays we would consider Doshie a stunner. She is small and has straight, shiny hair as black as pitch, so long it would hang below her waist, except that she always wears it up, wound in the most intriguing folds. She must have some Cherokee blood somewhere in her ancestry. She is timid and doesn't say much. In many ways she is as awkward and inexperienced as Myrtle Lee, but she moves with an unconscious grace far different from the clomping gait of her cousin.

And finally, there is Garlan, my father, who is a little older than the rest and really shouldn't be in the Hebron class. He won't play much of a role in this story, but he comes up in other ones, and I wanted you to meet him briefly in this setting. He is hanging around the Hebron class, by the way, just because of Doshie's glistening hair. He certainly has an eye for pretty girls.

There they are, the Hebron Sunday School class at Zion Springs Baptist Church in 1928. They gather at 9:45 every Sunday morning for Opening Assembly. The Sunday School superintendent A.V. Rutherford (everybody really calls him Rufford) will call for prayer requests in this Opening Assembly. The young Hebron class members, all lined up together on the back two rows, will hear about Zulie Putnam's baby daughter, whose brain has swelled up, about Ella Victoria Padgett's mother with a lung clot in Piedmont County Memorial Hospital, about Hessie's friend Grady Blanton who turned his Oldsmobile over in a ditch near Washburn Switch and has strained his back. They'll also hear from A.V. "Rufford" about the boll weevils that are an especial plague on the cotton this year.

I am afraid the young folks don't pay too much attention during the prayer requests, and especially during the prayer itself. A.V. Rutherford, when he prays, prays at great length. They no longer ask him to lead prayer in the 11:00 service because they'll be 1:00 getting out if he's called upon. But on this morning in 1928, the prayer requests are received, and the prayer takes place while the bored youngsters sneak messages to each other by pointing to the titles in the Baptist hymnal. Buford opens to "Abide with Me" and points it out to Doshie, who blushes. Addie Green finds "I Need Thee Every Hour" and makes Hilary turn red to the roots of his hair. When Assembly and the prayer requests are over, they all file into Miss Edna's class, to try to straighten out the difference in Elijah and Elisha (Miss Edna can never keep it straight) or why the angel Michael disputed with Satan over Moses's body. Miss Edna can never get that straight either, and from what I hear, neither can the theologians at Southern Seminary in Louisville, where Preacher Gordon studied.

FALL, 1944

Just over sixteen years have now gone by in the lives of the members of Miss Edna's Hebron Sunday School class. We are here on another bright Sunday morning. The war is going on in Europe. The newspaper, the *Piedmont Daily Star,* carries pictures of maps with fat, black arrows showing where Patton's tanks are thrusting through France toward Germany.

Myrtle Lee is the only one of Miss Edna's Sunday School class who has not married and had a family. She continues to wear cotton print dresses (a few sizes bigger) and is still dependent on Miss Dixie. I started to say she was still under the iron fist of Miss Dixie, but that wouldn't be fair, because Miss Dixie has done the best she could with a spineless husband and a big old lump of a girl for a daughter. "Big old lump of a girl." That's what Bate Hamrick calls her. Nowadays, in the 1990's, Myrtle Lee, as graceless as she was, would have been pregnant several times over, but there were no abortions in those days, and Miss Dixie guarded her big daughter's virtue as tightly as Patton defended his fuel supplies.

Lowell Megginson runs a little wooden grocery store and gas station over by Washburn Switch. He married Preacher Gordon's only daughter, Sarah. His brother Buford has done well. Sometime after 1940, Buford got obsessed with acquiring land, and when the war came he was able to really start accumulating acres, which he put in cotton, for the war effort. He married Doshie, who now has given birth to four of their five children, with a daughter still to come. Because of Buford's land purchases, he and Doshie moved over to the Mooresboro community, but they still cut across the county every Sunday for services at Zion Springs. Hessie has married Grady Blanton, who recovered nicely from his automobile accident years before, so that at least one prayer request of 1928 was answered for sure. Hessie and Grady have four daughters, Jorene, Carolene, Erlene, and Paulene, but they have never had the son that Grady craves. Grady is the only male in the group who went to war, and he will go through it all, earning medals at the Battle of the Bulge. Nine months after he returns from Europe, by the way, he and Hessie will finally have their son, whom they will name Haroldteen, after one of my cousins.

The popular and charming Addie Green has indeed won and married the promising Hilary Bridges. Hilary did go to Wake Forest, where he made all A's and went on to Southern Seminary and presumably straightened out Elijah and Elisha. Everybody predicted a great future for him somewhere in the Southern Baptist Convention, but maybe because of the war, he somehow has not moved up much in Baptist circles and still pastors a tiny, struggling little church outside Boiling Springs, North Carolina. He and Addie are welcomed as honored visitors this morning.

Garlan is long gone. He lost interest in Doshie after a few weeks and after a few threats from Buford, and went off to marry an Alabama girl. He now lives in Charlotte, where there are a lot of jobs because of the war.

The members of the Hebron class have been split up now. In the way of Baptist churches, the men go to one class and the women to another, but they still gather for assembly. A.V. Rutherford died of lung cancer and relieved them of his long-winded prayers back in 1938. His place has been taken by Tyree Padgett, a bald man, one of the managers at Dunlap Mills, and he's more modern, and a little briefer, but he still concludes each prayer, as did A.V., with the traditional formula, "Forgive us of our miny miny sins," so the Hebron tradition goes on.

There are only a couple of requests this morning, but one of them is especially serious to the Hebron group. Miss Edna in 1931 married a man named Povie Badgett. Povie and his brother Ryan were the only two members of Zion Springs to go overseas in the First World War, in 1918. Povie had seen some awful things in the trenches and came back what in those days they called shell shocked. He got over it, they thought, before he married Miss Edna, but when the Second World War started, it triggered something still in him. He would sit by the radio night after night and listen to reports of battles and losses. Occasionally he would see the names of places where he had suffered in the trenches in those maps on the front page of the *Daily Star*. Last Thursday night, he had gone out to the barn, carrying a shotgun. He took off one of his brogans, put the gun barrel in his mouth, and pressed the trigger with his big toe. Miss Edna, in the house with her little boy Baxter, had rushed out to the barn in her nightgown and found him lying in the straw.

Buford, Hilary and Lowell, Hessie, Addie, Doshie and Myrtle Lee, will in a moment close their eyes and pray for their former teacher, Miss Edna, who couldn't keep Elijah and Elisha straight, and who is now going to have to manage the Badgett farm and finish raising her boy Baxter by herself. If they choose to open their eyes during the prayer, they will be able to see Povie's grave, a fresh clay scar in the graveyard beside the church.

They will pray about the war, of course, that Grady will come back safe. He will, and I wish I could reassure Hessie, who cries at night for Grady sometimes, but that's not the way Prayer Requests work. She'll have to wait to see what the answer is. Hessie raises her hand and requests prayer for Jorene, Carolene, Erlene and Paulene, who all have the sniffles.

On this morning during the Opening Assembly, the war and Miss Edna's tragedy and the drippy noses are the only prayer requests.

There should be more requests, probably. Doshie's face is pinched and drawn. Buford hasn't been talking to her much for over a year now. During the days he is out in the fields, working cotton or plowing with his big tractor. "It's war work," he barks when she complains about his being away all the time. Poor Doshie doesn't know how to say, I want you to love me like you did when I was a slender young girl, and my hair shone in the moonlight. Even when Buford comes home in the evening, he just silently eats the supper she has fixed , and then he gets out his deeds to thumb over them and add up columns in his bank statements. I don't think Doshie knows the things troubling her can be prayed about by church folk. She just assumes she has done something wrong, and in her mortification keeps quiet.

And someone might well request prayer for Addie and Pastor Hilary. His stingy deacons are trying to fire him, and he and Addie are in bad shape financially. They are facing the possibility of having to sell the little farm she inherited from her folks. If they sell it, Buford will probably be the one to get it.

Old Man Ira Megginson, who is ancient by this time, is still around, although few people see him. He wound up quarreling with everybody, including gentle Preacher Gordon, who is now an invalid. Old Man Ira split with the present pastor over a question of whom Cain married when he was sent out from Adam and Eve's home. He is now living in a shack behind Hessie, who does her best for him, but it's difficult for her, seeing him so cut off from everybody. Hessie and Lowell know that he needs prayer, but they don't say so publicly.

None of these last matters are the kinds of things you can ask prayer about in the Opening Assembly in 1944, so I guess the people just hold them in their hearts and pray by themselves.

Lowell, humble Lowell, also has a secret prayer. He has never been a confident man, and these days he is feeling especially inadequate. He did not go to the war. He has never stood out in any way at all. When he looks around at the Hebron group, all he can see is how badly he has fallen short. Lowell, with sinking heart, believes that he has nothing to offer. He is a failure, for his country and his God. So as Tyree Padgett prays on behalf of the Opening Assembly, Lowell from the depths of his sense of unworthiness privately asks his Father, "Please, please make me useful to You. Let me live for You, do something for You."

All the former Hebron class members are moving into middle age and its cares, and if those uttered and unuttered prayer requests could be extracted from this small Zion Springs building and flashed to the world at large which is focused on the war and hoping for peace, many of the prayer requests might wind up discouraging everybody.

Such petitions display the shapes a fallen world takes on, whether there's a war or not.

FALL, 1991

This Sunday I have crossed the mountains from Tennessee and will attend Zion Springs Baptist Church in Piedmont County, North Carolina.

The church building is different now. The original structure with its distinctive white columns on the front porch has been torn down and replaced by a more modern, rectangular church house in red brick. There is an impressive white steeple on top. Now Zion Springs looks quite unsingular, just like all the other churches you see from North Carolina's highways.

A three-story education building has been constructed alongside the sanctuary, and it is to this building that I go for the Opening Assembly of the Senior Adult Sunday School. I haven't been there for a long time, not since Garlan's funeral.

My Uncle Lowell is the one in charge, the one who goes to the front, makes announcements about the cookout by the springs this afternoon and the Business Women's Breakfast next Friday. He also calls for the prayer requests.

He is still as slender as when he was a boy, but bald, and I know there is a pacemaker under the skin of his chest. His handsome, sensitive face is sad as he tells us that the former Addie Green died last Thursday and was buried in the city cemetery yesterday afternoon. Her husband, the former pastor Hilary Bridges, has had Alzheimer's for several years and is in a home near Ellenboro. When Hilary's son told him Addie was gone, he didn't remember who she was and asked for a piece of chewing gum.

Lowell also tells us that Myrtle Lee is in Piedmont Memorial Hospital, a big graceless figure lying in a bed. Miss Dixie died in 1987, leaving Myrtle Lee alone, and Lowell went by to check on her last Monday, as he does several times a week, and he found her unconscious on the kitchen floor. The doctors have removed part of her stomach.

Hessie raises her hand and asks prayer for Grady. Grady had made it back from the war safe and sound, and for years he drove an eighteen-wheeler for a company over in Swananoa. Hessie merely requests general prayer for him, but Lowell will tell me later that Grady is in the last stages of cancer. He will tell me in horror, "Yulan, it was like nothing I ever heard of. He told me his privates swelled up and exploded. He's been wounded in battle and has been through every kind of cancer operation, but he said this was the worst pain he'd ever had."

Tolliver Hamrick holds up his hand and requests prayer for Miss Edna. She is ninety now, still living alone because Baxter has been out in New Mexico for over thirty years because of his lungs. Tolliver had been driving by the Badgett place Tuesday past and had seen her stretched out on her back in the grass between the house and the barn. He'd pulled in and gone over to her. Her eyes were open. She had looked up at him brightly. "Just some dizziness," she said, and "I'm resting a spell." Baxter has come in from Albuquerque and they are looking for a lady to stay with her. "Pray for somebody good to be guided to her," Lowell suggests.

There is a long pause, and nobody presents any more requests. So Lowell himself asks prayer for Buford and Doshie. Doshie started having strokes eight years back, and by now she can't talk or communicate. All she can do is lie there in bed helpless, unable even to feed herself. Because she's bedridden, they finally were obliged to cut off all her long, shiny hair, the first time scissors had ever touched her head. They think she knew what was happening. She can't cry like normal folks, but they say her eyes closed and tears flowed down her cheeks when she heard the snipping.

Buford hasn't been able to take care of Doshie himself, not even at night when there's really nothing to do. Everybody says he just doesn't want to take care of her. His health is bad, and he is so scared of dying his kids sent him up to Morganton, where a psychiatrist had to put him on strong antidepressants. He cries all the time about dying. He calls Lowell every day. "Come over, Lowell, I'm dying. My heart's going. I know I'm dying."

Buford never even learned to boil water himself, and refuses to try, so he has had to hire nurses to take care of his wife. Buford can't even bring himself to moisten her mouth with wet Q-Tips when her tongue dries out. Nurses, of course, are expensive, three to four hundred dollars a day. As time has gone on, Buford has had to sell land. A parcel of 25 acres at first, then one of 47, then 75. Every acre of his land is now gone. He has even sold the old home to his son, and all he can do is look with despair at the inert Doshie and cry because he is afraid to die.

Doshie, of course, can't express her feelings, but occasionally the nurses say she will utter a high-pitched little squeal that sometimes goes on for hours. It sounds like something electronic, and about drives Buford crazy.

Finally, the prayer requests come to an end as Lowell adds prayer for his wife Sarah, whose knees were too swollen for her to make it to church this morning.

As I listen to the prayer requests, and watch Lowell, I can look out at the graveyard. I can see my parents' graves, my grandparents', A.V. "Rufford's," Miss Dixie's, all the others. I look past the rows of old heads in front of me and marvel at Lowell, who is presiding so modestly and competently over the Prayer Requests. Lowell, sensitive Uncle Lowell, had a few decades back appeared to be the most unremarkable of them all. He had begun with nothing of the intelligence of Hilary, or the fun loving charm of Addie, the sheer raw power of will of Buford, or the indestructible solidity of Myrtle Lee. He had lost his country grocery store and gas station twenty years before when a modern convenience mart moved in by Dunlap Mills. He had straightway gotten a job in the mill so he could take care of Sarah. He never complains. And now he is almost the only one, except for Hessie, still on his feet. Lean and in a handsome straw hat, Lowell takes care of anybody who seems to need him. He gets out to visit all the old Hebron class—those who are left—several times a week. He listens to their complaints and sits quietly while they talk about whatever is on their minds. The scripture has told him to tend the sick and the needy, and he does. With joy. Then he goes home to pray for them every night.

And now, of them all, he is the one up there in front during the Opening Assembly, taking the prayer requests. He told me once that back during the war, when he felt so down that he could barely raise his head, he had breathed a prayer to God. "I begged God to start using me, as worthless as I was."

As everybody bows their heads and Lowell prays for us, I reflect that Lowell's life proves that prayer requests do work, that God does answer our petitions.

I like going by Zion Springs Baptist Church in Piedmont County, North Carolina. I pass by there as often as I can. I stand at the foot of graves. I especially try to show up for prayer requests in the Opening Assembly, because prayer requests (uttered and unuttered) are how the news of life and death truly spreads among those in the Body of Christ.

Reprise

In English, the word "hero" does not refer just to those who are famous, whose great deeds influence masses of people. Personages like Plato, Charles Dickens, Winston Churchill, Eleanor Roosevelt, Mother Teresa, Billy Graham and Bill Clinton possess names which have been made famous by the world.

But the English language, in its wisdom, does not limit the use of the word "hero" to those who have achieved fame. English allows the word "hero" also to be used for the central figure of any drama or story. We talk about the "hero" of a play or novel. Oliver Twist is the hero of a famous novel. George Bailey is the hero of a film called "It's a Wonderful Life."

In this sense, all people, all of us, are called by our Lord to become heroes. You and I will never be famous in the world's eye, but we are heroes in God's dramas, with plots drafted in heaven itself. God is among us, working out His precious stories. His are all stories of love, of success and failure in love, here in time, under the sun.

He will honor His heroes in Eternity, when both time and the sun are no more.

Up Home

A large, white frame house not far from Zion Springs Baptist Church occupies an honored place in my remembrance. A broad flight of cement steps welcomed all comers to the dwelling, which was wrapped in porches on three sides. Wooden rocking chairs formed a row on the front porch, and a creaking swing hung from chains fixed to the slatted porch ceiling. The line of the green shingled roof was broken by various interesting angles and gables, as was fashionable at the time the house was constructed before the First World War. A hall with rooms opening off each side led straight from the front door to the back exit. In the rear of the house, another large porch, screened-in, sheltered a well, and was ample enough to serve as overflow space for family reunions or church socials. There was a smoke house a few convenient paces from the kitchen door. Two old unpainted barns rose at the edge of the woods behind the house. A pair of outhouses, a double for the family and a single for the servants who occasionally worked in the house or fields, was discreetly spaced between the two barns.

An orchard of damson trees, peaches and pears sheltered one side of the big white house, and the dirt road to Lattimore outlined the tiny orchard, separating it from Ray Bankhead's cotton field. The front lawn sloped down to Zion Springs Switch Road, an asphalt two-laner, and four magnificent oaks graced the area with their shade. Paralleling the paved road, the Southern Railway ran its line, providing passenger service to nearby towns and a siding for the unloading of one hundred- pound sacks of feed and guano for the farmers who were the backbone of the little community and its churches.

Preacher Gordon and his wife Ella bought this home from Gordon's Uncle Chance when he moved to Waycross, Georgia in 1916 and raised their children in it. Their fairly numerous brood had set down roots with their own families in the fields and towns round about.

Garlan and Georgia, caught in one of the emergencies of the first unsatisfactory years of their marriage, came to live in one of the home's bedrooms for a year or two. A baby bed was set up for me in one corner. Even after my family moved out to a duplex apartment in the county seat seven miles away, Garlan and Georgia never ceased to return often to the big house. It remained an attraction and comfort to them, probably because the purity of Preacher Gordon's and Ella's life together represented a stability that contrasted with the ups and downs of the experimental way of living which the young couple and their generation had fallen into.

Garlan and Georgia called the place "Up Home." Almost every weekend, they would inform my brother and me, "We're going up home," which to us meant the delights of homemade ice cream, piles of Ella's tea cakes, endless fried chicken, an occasional treat of squirrel or rabbit—the gift of members of Preacher Gordon's congregation—and the thrill of screaming and stomping romps around the porches with country cousins galore.

I have two memories of the bedroom my parents lived in Up Home, both bittersweet.

When I was a toddler, both my parents suffered from gastric problems, although I as a self-absorbed pre-schooler was not aware of them, and certainly not aware that I might be the cause of some of them. What I was aware of was that they regularly consumed X-lax, a sweet chocolate laxative. I saw them leave a package of it one summer day on the mantel above the fireplace in our room. When they left me alone, I quickly got a straight back wooden chair, shoved it next to the mantel, climbed up, reached high with my short arms, and the treasure was mine. I ate it all. It was delicious, all the more so since I had gotten it on my own, and they had been incomprehensibly stingy, keeping it to themselves. Afterwards, I wandered into the big kitchen with its black wood stove. My Aunt Sarah turned from a steaming pot and saw on my messy mouth the evidence of what I had accomplished. She questioned me sharply. I was smug: "Candy good." When Georgia was told, she called Dr. Bridges, who informed her that I would not die from it, but that she would probably think I was going to die if something were not done quickly. I remember riding to the hospital. I was small enough to stand in the front seat (as was common for little children in those days), watching the fields race by our black Dodge, pleased that I had not only gotten the candy but was receiving a lot of attention as well.

I was not pleased by the attention I got at the hospital. Attendants slapped me down on a gurney, inserted tubes down my nose and washed out my stomach. I drummed my heels furiously on the gurney pad, and yelled with all my strength.

The second memory has to do with another summer and another medical crisis. When I was sixteen, I was on an extended visit Up Home and developed a cold which would not go away. The diagnosis was rheumatic fever, which ran in the family. My heart swelled alarmingly (I could see it clearly, thumping under the skin covering my ribs), and I had to be checked frequently at the local clinic. Complete rest was ordered, and I was put to bed in the same room where I had eaten the laxative. I was a compliant patient, quite good-natured about my condition, but as time went on and I was told over and over by the doctor and his nurses that I could live as long as anyone if I took care of myself, I began to realize that the reassurances implied that I also might <u>not</u> live as long as anyone. When orders were issued that I was to give up sports and do no more physical exertion, I read up on the disease and was depressed by what I learned. I was not left in fear of imminent death, but I assumed until I was in my twenties that my life would likely be shortened, that I would probably survive only into my late thirties or forties. Having the end of life press so close was hard knowledge for a teenager to bear, and it changed me. Reading became my all consuming passion since outdoor exertions were forbidden me.

The rambling old house figures in other important moments of my life. It was Preacher Gordon who from this house, before I was born, bequeathed to me my odd name. He and Ella had had a string of boys, and it was one of their rare whimsies to endow each one of them with a name terminating in the letters -an: Waylan, Herman, Rayman, Garlan and Ryan. Ryan, by the way, died when quite young. He was born sickly, and his big brothers despised him because they were charged by their busy mother with looking after him while she worked over the wood stove at apple pies and hot cornbread, or canning, or with the other women boiled clothes in black, cast-iron pots on wash day in the yard space between the house and the barns. The colicky baby cried most of the time, irritating his young caretakers. One of the brothers, who will remain nameless, told me he remembered spitting angrily in Ryan's open mouth and wishing he would die on one occasion as the child wailed, his mouth a little "o." By the way, Ryan's tombstone is to be found in Zion Springs graveyard, a few feet from that of the sibling who privately felt more terrible than anyone else at his little brother's funeral and carried for six decades afterward the guilt of what he had done.

But Preacher Gordon and Ella wanted a girl, whom they would name Sarah Louise, to honor his mother and hers, so they tried once more for what they hoped would be their last child. Since they had prayed over the matter, they were surprised when the baby showed up as a boy, requiring another name ending in -an. The only other such name in the community which they knew of was Wyan, and neither parent liked the name. Preacher Gordon had a large personal library and had run across the exotic word "yulan" in one of his books. It was transliterated from Chinese, designating a delicate white orchid, not entirely suitable for a robust male baby, but both Gordon and Ella liked the sound of the word, so they used it as the name for the infant, and tried once more for the longed for little girl, who answered their prayers a couple of years afterward.

This last son turned out to be the pick of the male litter to the preacher and his wife. All of the other sons had a wild youth and brought some form of scandal or disappointment into their lives, but not Yulan. He was a compliant, untroublesome child and universally admired, even by his rapscallion brothers. He was the only one of the boys to go to college, and emerged a respected medical doctor. His name was passed on to me, in hopes that I would not be as wild and untamable as my paternal uncles had proved to be.

Preacher Gordon was famous for his sense of service to anybody who was in need, and the white house saw many anguished members of his congregation knock on its doors. In the dark days of the 1920's he co-signed bank notes for farmers in his congregation, and when the depression hammered Piedmont County with its hard blows, he lost most of the land which had been his pride and his occupation. Even as his modest wealth was dwindling, however, he put out money for an automobile because it would allow him to serve the dispersed members of his congregation better. Unfortunately, he never learned to drive the vehicle, except into ditches. Everyone feared to see him coming down the narrow and ill-kept clay roads, weaving and crashing gears. When my parents came to live with him, he nobly gave up driving, and my mother, an excellent little speedster who had learned to scoot around Alabama roads which were even worse than those of Piedmont County, North Carolina, drove him everywhere. She of course had to take me with her, and family members tell me that I must have been to a hundred funerals before I was five years old. Except for one brief memory of topping some Piedmont County hill, and seeing a white church steeple spiring out of the sloping cotton fields and pastures in front of us, I remember nothing of those funeral trips. I was in my late teens, however, before I could learn to feel anything but repulsion at the whiff of fresh flowers.

I was Up Home and one of those in the kitchen with Preacher Gordon the day he had his massive stroke. Four years old, I was making my way through a midday plateful of green beans laced with fatback, white corn and Irish potatoes, and anticipating a tea cake as my reward. He leaned against the doorjamb of the pantry and began to chuckle hoarsely in a sinister way. I thought he was teasing me. I don't remember what happened next, but Aunt Sarah tells me that she ran to get Dr. Yulan, who happened to be visiting and was out by the smoke house smoking with Waylan. I believe I quietly remained at the table waiting for my tea cake while the alarmed adults got their father out of the kitchen and into a car for the trip to Piedmont County Memorial Hospital. I suppose my Aunt Sarah stayed home and gave me my dessert, which I deserved, since I had cleaned up my plate.

The next time I saw Preacher Gordon he was a paralyzed old man, and his wonderful intelligence had been snuffed out. All of his children faithfully took care of him, but the lot of prime caregivers fell to his daughter Sarah and her husband Lowell. For the rest of his life, he spent his nights in his own bed and most of his days in a rocking chair in front of a coal fire in the grate of his bedroom. When they got him up, his left arm dangled useless, and his left foot dragged. The only words he had the power to utter were, "Ah, pshaw," which he expostulated when he was being teased or told something extraordinary. Every time we went up home, I watched his decline with awe.

When he died seven years later, his coffin was placed in his own bedroom, across the hall from where we slept. Countless visitors flocked to his house to honor him and bid him goodbye. My parents and I spent the nights before the funeral in our accustomed bedroom. I knew my grand-father lay a short distance away in his coffin, my imagination ran wild, and I was afraid.

Other affecting memories crowd my remembrance of the house.

The parlor at the front of the home provided many unforgettable scenes. It was the first room you entered after climbing the front steps and crossing the porch. The room was not especially large, and was carpeted and filled with big overstuffed chairs. An upright piano, which is now in the dining room of my Aunt Sarah's house on Albert Blanton Road, was the center of many family sings, for we were famous for our music. One key memory stands out for me: the time my Uncle Yulan (he was Big Yulan and I was Little Yulan, to avoid confusion) surprised me by singing "Drink to Me Only with Thine Eyes," and dedicating the song to the little boy who was his namesake.

Another memory of the parlor is more dire. I was three years old, and my cousin Haroldteen, one of Lowell and Sarah's boys, was a little older than I, and much bolder. Every time a train passed he would bang the parlor's screen door, dash down the cement front steps, and run to the edge of the lawn by the paved road, to stand under the twin oaks and wave at the engineer, who delighted him by always waving back. I was terrified of the noise and power of the big engines, even though they fascinated me. I was too cowardly to accompany Haroldteen, but I had figured out that trains could not get through screen doors. Every day, when the train passed, Haroldteen would assume his station at the edge of the yard, and I would plaster my nose to the protecting screen door and regard in awe both the powerful, huffing locomotive and my cousin's courage. One afternoon I watched as a white hound dog, a big creature with large brown spots, slunk swiftly across the lawn, looping around the big trees. I can recall the animal behind Haroldteen, raising its front paws onto his hips. That is the last thing I remember seeing. Some now erased horror made me squeeze my eyes tightly shut and begin to scream, drumming my feet up and down on the wooden floor of the parlor in terror. The animal was rabid and the attack must have been vicious. Aunt Sarah came running. Her cries brought a colored man who had been eating hoop cheese and crackers on a bench outside my uncle's country store. He grabbed up fistfuls of sand and cast it into the dog's eyes, fearlessly driving the animal away from my cousin, who was bleeding in his shoulders and hips. A farmer with a shotgun killed the dog before it could escape. My next memory is when my aunt took me down to the store so that I could see the dead beast sprawled as if asleep in the back of a pickup truck. My final memory of the episode is the evening of the attack when the adults burned Haroldteen's striped bib overalls and jacket in the fireplace and talked of the dreadful long needle which would penetrate my cousin's stomach thirty-two times during the weeks when he would receive his anti rabies shots.

Many other remembrances of the old house remain within me. I recall the time when I was four years old, and Santa Claus brought me a little bow and arrow, a tomahawk, and an Indian headdress. I don't recall a single thing I did with the toys, but I do recall my pride in them, even though I must have made a ridiculous little figure. In fact, I know I made a queer little character, because my mother took a photograph of me at the time, and stored it away in a box which I now possess. I also remember the occasion when I was given a few pennies to buy ice cream at my uncle's store and lost them in the sandy path leading from the house to the store. My mother put aside her chores and went searching with me for the money, the tip of her slipper stirring the sand here and there while I anxiously trailed her. When we failed to find what I had lost, she replaced the little coppers, and I ran happily to my uncle and purchased a popsicle. Etched within me are memories of a slaughtered hog and its hideous smell as it was being dressed by the women. The sight of the beast, as white as snow stretched out on a wooden skiff for dismemberment, is still vivid.

Finally, I recall standing naked in a dishpan on the back porch one evening at dusk as my mother gave me a bath. A screech owl called in a distant tree beyond the orchard, alarming me, but the porch was screened and my mother was there, so I knew it could not get me. It is perhaps my earliest memory.

Much of my life has been built upon foundations laid in that old house. The comfort, security, country feasts, fun with innumerable cousins, and the love of my grandparents and of Sarah and Lowell, who brimmed with pride in my accomplishments in high school and my honors in the university —these experiences established me, and are a part of my breeding. The old place and the people who made it their home are the source of my being and probably of my salvation.

Up Home is nothing but memory now. Sometime in the late 1960's, my aunt and uncle sold the land to a manufacturing company, and the new owners needed a place for their workers to park their cars. It was decided to put the empty structure to the torch. In an outburst of civic spirit, the company invited the fire department from a nearby town to use the destruction of the site as a practice exercise. The firemen came and burned it down. The local newspaper gave a short news item to the conflagration, the old home's single encounter with celebrityhood.

I have refused to read that news item.

I learned many things at the home where Preacher Gordon and Ella lived and died. Whatever capacity for love I possess, was born there. But the main thing I carry with me from Up Home is the sense, deep inside me, that even a secure refuge on this earth is subject to invasion by death and tragedy, that the captains of strongholds will lie in state in their banquet hall, that serpents will besiege even the inhabitants of Eden.

Chronicles of the Appeal:

God Calls His Children
In the Splendid Language of
Sign & Event

Apples & Bread & the Language of God

...comfort me with apples....
Song of Solomon

The book of Genesis begins with two extremely interesting notions. The first is that man is made in the image of God. The second is that one of man's primordial tasks was to give a name to each animal.

This means that God uses language, just as the creature fashioned in His image does.

Another arresting notion of Genesis is that God used a fruit (the apple, according to human tradition) to teach man the eternal purpose for which he was created. Obedience, love and death were thus linked by a commonplace fruit as ingredients of destiny.

The following true account provides evidence that God still uses everyday foods and little events to draw men and women toward Himself.

Amanda and Abby were two friends in Knoxville, Tennessee who, in the first part of their lives, were very much daughters of Eve. I will not distract the reader by describing how these women were deaf to the language of God when they were teenagers and young adults. Each, like her ancestress, succumbed to the temptations specific to her era and situation. Each also turned to God when she had been broken by life. Each was lifted toward nobility of character as she accepted the lesson that love is a discipline, that love in the profoundest sense involves obedience to God, even in the seemingly most inconsequential matters.

The two young women were brought together at a turning point in their lives. Amanda was living in a cheap apartment complex with Wesley, her truck driver husband, and Emma, their seven year old little girl. Abby was the resident manager, living with her husband and her son, Bobby, who was the same age as Emma. Amanda and Abby became fast friends.

Both marriages were troubled. In time, Amanda and Wesley found their divisions being slowly and painfully healed, in the most miraculous way. In the fires of redemption, their quarrels and bitterness toward one another were transmuted. As their spirits grew in generosity, so did their prosperity. They were able to move into their own home, a modest but well made dwelling which they decorated intentionally so that it would exemplify to visitors their devotion to God and the hard-won joy of their union.

About a year after Amanda left the apartment complex, Abby told her that she was frightened. Some kind of growth was swelling her tongue, causing considerable pain. She was afraid to go to the doctor about it. When, at Amanda's insistence, she screwed up her courage and went in for a diagnosis, she received the dreadful news that the swelling was cancerous. Later the doctors would shock her still more by telling her that her cancer was of a particularly malignant sort.

Every part of Abby's life immediately began to disintegrate. As she underwent treatments of radiation and chemotherapy, her unstable relationship with her husband could not bear the stress. He left. Abby found herself on her own with a mortal disease, and a little son to raise.

Abby was of a naturally heroic spirit, and when she and Amanda met to talk about their lives, she displayed her fighting mettle. Each time she fell into depression over what was happening to her—the treatments, the pain, the drugs, the loneliness, and fear—she always bounced back, recovering both her sense of humor and her bright images of the future, however limited that future might be.

In time, however, it became clear she could no longer fight her battles without practical daily help. Although the owners of the apartment complex where she was employed supported her loyally, she realized that she was unable to do the work which a good manager was responsible for. She also could not in these circumstances properly care for her son. There were too many hospitalizations, too much pain which drove her inside herself. Abby gave up her life in the southern city where she had gone to seek her fortune. She fled back to Virginia, where her mother, Cindy, could join her in her final battles.

Abby moved into a little house a block from her mother's, and the two women deliberately began to structure the little boy's life to prepare him for the coming years when he would live entirely without his mother. Abby spent as much time with Bobby as she could, showing him how delighted with him she was, but as the months passed and Abby was frequently in the hospital or too debilitated by her disease to take care of him, his grandmother was transferred more and more responsibility for his care.

Amanda and Abby maintained contact. Abby sometimes traveled to Knoxville, and the two friends would meet. As time went on, Abby's treatments became more and more drastic. Portions of her tongue and most of her lower jaw were surgically removed. She was sent to Texas for operations which, while they could not cure her, could proportion her a few extra months of life. Her mother and son went with her, to be of comfort to her, but soon Abby had to reveal to them from her bed that they were hearing her voice for the last time: her vocal chords were to be removed. Her mother, who loved her daughter's silvery lilt, could barely stand to end the conversation, knowing that her little girl's voice was shortly to be silenced forever. Bobby, since the mother and daughter were sparing him, did not fully understand, but the next time he saw his mother, she could no longer talk to him.

Amanda learned of what had happened to Abby's voice when she got a telephone call from Texas. It was an operator, who explained that she was speaking on behalf of a party who could not talk. Abby would type what she wanted to communicate into a computer linked to the phone. The operator would relay what was on her screen to Amanda. Amanda realized with shock that she would never hear Abby speak again.

"Can Abby hear me now?" Amanda choked out to the operator.

"No, she can't. She can only hear me," the operator replied.

"Good," Amanda told her, "because I've got to stop and cry this out before we can go on."

Amanda's car was so old that she could not make the trip to Virginia often to see her dying friend, but her and Wesley's extensive group of friends and church supporters made sure that the two women were not left bereft of one another as Abby entered her last days. From time to time, one of them would drive Amanda up for a few hours visit.

Abby's appearance was shocking. It was not just the baldness and pallor. The doctors had reconstructed a substitute for the bottom part of her face. A large trache hole exposed the inner workings of her throat, and the skin of her neck was permanently blackened. Her breasts were removed to provide fatty tissue for tube openings and facial reconstruction. What the surgeons had cobbled together was better than a gaping jaw, but their best efforts left her looking freakish.

Abby was desperate to stay alive. She submitted to whatever procedures might grant her extra weeks of life. When she could no longer eat, food was introduced by tube directly into the stomach. When her tongue and part of the esophagus proved spotted with new cancer, they were removed. Malnourishment left the remains of her face drawn and thin. She came to be cadaverously skinny. In the last months of her life, Abby got to the point that she could no longer stand the tube feeding. She learned to pour milk shakes directly down the stump of her esophagus, something which the doctors had told her would be impossible. Such nourishment became one of her few pathetic physical gratifications as she moved toward her end.

Although Amanda in some ways dreaded every visit to see her dying friend, each visit turned out to be a source of joy. Amanda talked, and Abby wrote notes to her like an excited schoolgirl. They talked about the things that all young women talk about, their children and families and housekeeping. On one occasion, Amanda asked Abby what she wanted to talk about. Abby scribbled, "Romance!"

Amanda marveled at the way Abby decorated her house so that it would be bright and pleasant for her son. Her kitchen was especially beautiful, an expression of life, of bounty and joy. Its motif was apples. Apples were everywhere—on the drying cloth, the counter top, the wallpaper. Pictures of apples adorned the refrigerator.

The two friends were Christian and of course talked about death. They wept together at the sadness of what was happening. Abby had a firm belief that she would go to heaven when she died, even though she felt great distress that she was leaving her son behind to grow up without her. Amanda was a singer and a writer of songs. She encouraged her friend with her music and words. Once, when Amanda was acutely missing Abby's voice, she burst out:

"Abby, I have a picture in my mind of you standing before the Lord Jesus Himself, singing to Him. He smiles and claps His hands." Both young women's eyes sparkled at the prospect of the voiceless, tongueless Abby, her dark hair restored and her head thrown back, her throat smooth and undisfigured, singing rapturously before the throne of God, while angels and saints applaud jubilantly on the sidelines.

Even though Amanda wanted to minister faithfully to her friend, her own life was challenging her, sometimes crowding thoughts of Abby to the sidelines. She and her husband had grown loving and thoughtful to one another—Amanda almost felt guilty that she possessed the kind of relationship which Abby had irrevocably lost—but his work as a long-distance trucker was punctuated with layoffs. They were worrisomely stressed about money. It was this financial problem which brought Amanda one of her first contacts with the strange language which God employs with His children.

In a period of layoff after Christmas, the couple ran out of money. Although they had stocked beans and rice and canned goods for just such an emergency, they would have only $25.00 in cash for all their expenses over the next three weeks. And they had no bread. Since they were in the habit of praying, they held hands and asked that their funds somehow stretch far enough for them to avoid actual want.

Bread, however, they would have to have. They knew of a store which featured bread at cut-rate prices, so the little family piled noisily into their old car, good-naturedly trying to make an adventure out of their privation. They drove down to the end of their street and turned right. They proceeded for half a mile to Pleasant Ridge Road, a main cross-town street. They turned right and then left, following the grounds of a little neighborhood grammar school.

All of a sudden, by the entrance to the drive into the school grounds, they saw six loaves of bread lying ahead of them in the road. Both their jaws fell slack. They could scarcely believe their eyes. Wesley looked at his wife.

"Would you mind if I stopped and checked?" he asked. Amanda nodded, mystified.

Wesley pulled to a halt in the middle of the road, just short of the brightly colored packages. He jumped out and gathered up four loaves of the bread. In the car, the couple and their daughter examined the treasure: Merita Bread. The packaging seemed to be intact. Dared they eat bread found in a road? Where had it come from? A bakery truck leaving the grammar school? Awed and excited, they decided to take home the four loaves they had and leave the other two for someone else.

It happened that they were having guests that night. Amanda, without saying anything, served the bread with the meal. One of their guests, who had had dental work that day and was sore mouthed, commented on how thoughtful they were to serve such bread, so soft and fresh.

The rest of the loaves they froze and used until Wesley's next paycheck. Amanda took the strange experience and treasured it in her heart.

Early in January, Amanda visited Abby for what would turn out to be the last time. In the kitchen, in the midst of apples, they conversed, Amanda talking and Abby writing notes as fast as she could pen them. By this time, Abby's pain was so bad that she was living off morphine, expensive stuff which was being purchased for her by donations from members of Cindy's church. But Abby had not lost her optimism. She made plans to travel down to Knoxville to spend a few days at Amanda's home the next week.

She also dropped a small bombshell: she proposed spending the first part of the next week with a man she knew there. His name was Charlie. Her last two days in town she would come stay with Amanda. She would get in touch with Amanda from Charlie's to make arrangements after she got into town.

As Amanda made the trip home, she was much preoccupied. For the first time she understood Abby's reference to "romance" a couple of months earlier. Lots of half memories and allusions, remarks that had puzzled her, clicked into place in Amanda's mind. She was uneasy.

Monday came: no Abby. Tuesday passed, then Wednesday. No word from Abby.

Amanda, afraid that Abby had gotten sick, called Cindy. Cindy was surprised. "Abby has been in Knoxville since Sunday. She told me she was staying with you."

Amanda, assuming Cindy knew about Abby's plans to spend time with Charlie, explained the arrangements to her. Cindy was dismayed. Abby had kept her full Knoxville plans secret from her mother.

"Abby has taken up with this boyfriend. He has been a drug addict for years. I am frightened to death of him," Cindy cried. "He's a clever man. I worry about his influence on her and on the boy. She has just taken him totally into her life. Amanda, she tells me she thinks she can help him! He claims he is fighting his drug habit, but I am afraid he attached himself to Abby because she has access to morphine."

As Amanda listened to Abby's mother, she herself grew more and more agitated. Charlie had a history of instability and deviousness, of using anyone he met. Yet Abby was dazzled. That a man could still be interested in her, with her face and body ravaged, and her muteness! Cindy believed her daughter's judgment had flown out of the window. The relationship was coming between Abby and her mother.

Amanda talked by phone with Wesley, who more than shared her uneasiness. He had known many drug addicts. "We love Abby," he said, "but we don't want that guy in our home with you and Emma there by yourselves. Invite Abby, but not him. She can meet her boyfriend elsewhere.

"My own guess is that you won't even see Abby. He'll make sure that she doesn't leave him. He'll want to keep her away from normal people, keep her where he can maintain influence over her. Drug addicts are very controlling, especially when a lot is at stake for them."

Amanda found a mutual acquaintance who knew where Abby was staying and sent word that she badly wanted to see Abby, but alone.

From that time forward, Abby dropped her old friend. She actually spent time late in the week with a friend who lived only two blocks from Amanda's house, but she pointedly snubbed Amanda.

Only when she was leaving town to return to Virginia did she drop by to see Amanda for five minutes. Abby made it clear that she was carrying out nothing more than an obligatory social call. It was a cold visit, a visit of dismissal, worse to Amanda than no time together at all.

Amanda wept in bitter sorrow over the rupture, over the sad pain of the whole confusing situation.

A few days after Abby had made her visit and returned to Virginia, Amanda received a phone call on a Sunday morning in late January.

Abby was dead. She had strangled to death in the early hours of the morning, after trying to drink something. She had died struggling to operate her aspirator in order to clear the fluid which was choking her windpipe. Bobby had found his mother's body when he got up. The little boy telephoned 911, as he had been trained to do. Then he called his grandmother. Amanda was also told that Abby had planned another trip from Virginia to Knoxville for the following day.

She was coming down to marry Charlie.

Amanda was plunged into grief. She had loved Abby deeply. Yet less than two weeks before Abby died, their friendship had broken up. Abby had shut her out completely from what remained of her life. Now death had closed off forever any possibility of reconciliation.

Amanda spent most of that Sunday alone with Emma. Wesley was several states away in his truck and could not be with her. Emma, sensitive to her mother's troubled spirit, gave her time to herself. Amanda tried turning to God, but she was so upset that she could not pray, could not even give God her tears.

Well into the afternoon, many hours after she had received the news of Abby's death, Amanda realized that she had not remembered at all one of her most cherished memories of being with Abby, the memory of the times when they had talked bravely about Abby singing before the throne of God. Was she so angry at Abby for abandoning her, so wrapped up in her guilts about refusing to allow Abby to bring her unsuitable boyfriend to her home, that her mind had pushed aside this precious moment of union they had shared? Was she condemned to feel only loss and hopelessness and blankness at Abby's passing? Why was God not helping her? Why was there not one drop of consolation from heaven?

Wesley telephoned Amanda Monday night from a distant city, and in her brokenness Amanda spewed out her feelings about Abby and death and God. Even though Wesley was at a public telephone in Wal-mart, he told his wife he wanted to pray for her. She listened, glued to the phone, as his detailed prayer touched on every thought and feeling that had troubled her, even things she had not revealed to him. It was as if some angel had delivered the secrets of her heart to him, and he held them up to God for her, since she could not do it herself. The main request he raised to God was that she be able herself to go honestly to God, telling Him every confusion and anger and doubt that was in her heart. The next time they talked, she told him that nobody had ever prayed for her that way, that he must have been anointed in his prayer.

"That's exactly what everybody in Wal-mart said," he told her dryly.

Tuesday morning, almost forty-eight hours after she had received notice of Abby's death, Amanda was finally able to pray. She poured out directly to God all her hurt feelings, the doubt and guilt that were troubling her.

"I thought I loved Abby so much, Lord, but I am afraid now that I was fooling myself. Maybe what I felt was just sympathy, even a degrading self-importance that I was close to someone who was going to die. When I painted in my mind that picture of Abby, healed and whole and singing in her silvery voice before You, was I being a romantic, sentimental fool? Was I pretending, deceiving myself and Abby? Was the singing image I used to comfort her sent from You through me for her benefit, or was it just a cheap illusion of my foolish, posturing heart?"

Then, in her prayer, Amanda made a direct petition to God, which she herself was afraid must be outrageous, but which she felt compelled to make. "Lord, I must know about what has happened, about my love for Abby, if it was real, and my relationship to You, if it is real. If I was a silly child when I talked about Abby delighting You with her song, let me know. I want to change, to be more realistic, if that is what I should be.

"I have even doubted if Abby is with You. I need to know that she did not sacrifice her salvation by wandering away from You in the last days of her life on earth. If Abby has sung before You, has truly delighted You the way she and I imagined, I want You to let me know by sending me an apple. I want an apple, Lord. I don't want just any apple, green or yellow. I want a red apple, like those I have seen in Abby's kitchen. When I receive a red apple, I will know that I have not been foolish. I will know that Abby has been before You, that she is saved, and that my words to her about singing to You were true and real."

When Amanda stood up from her prayer, she could scarcely believe that she had been so bold as to pray in that fashion. Yet she felt utterly at peace, so at peace, in fact, that if nothing about an apple ever happened, she would not feel any distress. Maybe her prayer had been presumptuous, even irreligious. Nonetheless, her heart was at rest. Abby had died. Abby had been saved by the blood of Christ. Amanda felt no doubts, and the rupture between her and her friend seemed to have lost the importance it had previously had.

Amanda went through her day. She took Emma to school. She visited a friend, but without telling her anything about her prayer. Amanda ironed. All during the day she thought with awe of the preposterous prayer she had felt compelled to make. She did not really expect an answer. She was even rather embarrassed about what she had prayed, about how she had in a way tried to put God on the spot.

And of course, as the hours went by, nothing happened.

She picked up Emma after school. They played games and did some projects, and Emma was glad to have her mom back again from the absorption of confusion and intense grief.

By the time evening came, Amanda had given up any expectation she might have nourished that God would answer so quickly a prayer that was, she herself admitted, rather cheeky. At six o'clock, she and Emma went out to McDonald's as a treat to themselves. They would spread a big towel on the floor of the den when they got back and have themselves a picnic. It was twilight when they drove up in their driveway. Carrying their McDonald's bags, they went up the front steps. Amanda got out her keys. She opened the screen door. She looked down.

Two objects had been left between the screen door and the main door to the house. One of the objects was an envelope from the leader of Emma's Girl Scout troop.

The other object was a brown bag filled with apples. Six of them, as in the loaves of bread. Red apples.

Emma loves to describe what happened to her mother at this moment. She says that when her mom looked down, she drew back and gasped. Emma was alarmed. "What's the matter, Momma?"

Only when her mother burst out laughing was Emma reassured. She was even more reassured when Amanda, staring intently at the doorway, continued to laugh, winding up with a broad, slightly foolish smile on her face and astonishment lingering in her eyes.

Amanda and Emma gathered up the items in the doorway and went inside.

Amanda was too consumed with curiosity to start on their McDonald's feast. Who had delivered the apples? She had to know! As the hungry Emma looked on impatiently, Amanda called the scout leader, thinking that maybe she had brought the brown plastic bag at the same time she had dropped off the envelope. No one answered the phone at the scout master's house. Amanda next telephoned Irene, a Bethesda friend who was accustomed to bring her surprise gifts. Irene knew nothing about the sack of red apples.

"Let's eat, Momma," Emma said.

Amanda was ransacking her brain for possibilities. Who was the source of that wonderful gift behind her screen door, more wonderful than its givers had any idea of? She could not rest until they knew what they had been a part of, how the God of the universe had directly used them. She could think of no one who might be the donor.

As a last resort before giving up, Amanda decided to ask Howard and Ruth, the couple who lived next door, if they had seen anybody take a package up to her house. They were much older than Amanda and Wesley, but they had become good neighbors. They kept an eye on things when Amanda was out. Amanda rang them up and asked.

"I am so glad you liked the apples," Ruth answered immediately. "We thought you would."

"I'm coming over," Amanda exulted. "I have something huge to tell you!"

She grabbed Emma and dragged her away from the hamburgers, herding her out of the door. "Emma, you've got to hear this!" she laughed to her daughter, who was enjoying the excitement, even though she obviously thought her mother had gone pleasantly crazy.

The older couple smiled at the two bouncing figures on their doorstep, although mystified at such a reaction to a simple neighborly act.

"We had picked up a box of apples, more than we could use ourselves. We got to thinking you might want some. I took them over, but no one was at home. I left them behind the screen."

Amanda sat them down and recounted the whole story of Abby and her own desperate prayer. They were as thrilled by what had happened as she was. And Emma, who now was hearing the full story for the first time, was beaming from ear to ear, her hunger momentarily forgotten.

Amanda and Emma, after their time of rejoicing with their amazed neighbors, returned home. They carefully spread out a white towel on the den floor, the way they had planned, as a site for their picnic with warmed-over Big Mac's and slightly sodden French fries. Between them, in the middle of their improvised table cloth, they placed one red apple, and exulted over it as they ate and marveled.

For their part, Howard and Ruth shook their heads in awe all evening long that the Lord had used them to relay such an important communication. What had been for them a casual impulse of generosity had been transmuted by God into an expression of His personal love which they knew with joy would comfort not just Amanda, but everyone who heard of it.

And so it has been. The fruit which in the beginning marked alienation between God and His children was re-employed to signify His delight in the salvation of His daughters. Some who hear the story think of Abby who wandered away from God in the wild temptations of her last trials, and yet was found and again embraced against her Father's heart. Others discover in the bag of red apples as opposed to the one red apple of Amanda's request a sign that Abby has sung not just once, but many times since the morning of her earthly passing. Some people see the timing of Abby's death as a blessed rescue from adding an evil relationship to the unspeakable physical ordeal she was enduring, one that had already cost her closeness with her mother and friend at the time she needed them most.

But the main lesson of Amanda's bread and apples is that God speaks to His sons and daughters, and He does it in a variety of lively idioms. His bright lexicons are richer and simpler than human beings can conceive. Amanda was singled out in an amazing way, but so are we all. God's advents are tailored to the heart and life and circumstances of each of us, and He comes in such customized fashion because love is by its nature personal, God's love for us as well as our love for one another.

Abby's lost silvery voice now witnesses to Amanda with a fullness which nothing she ever dreamed of could have brought about alone.

And Abby witnesses to us too! The rapture of singing for the delight of God! What in the many languages of our Creator could be better than apples and bread to fortify us in this difficult life, to show us that concerts of majesty are the wondrous destiny of each of God's children?

Philip

I will never pretend that I understand love. Love is too vast, too incomprehensible for us fully to take in its nature and its meaning for us. Love is a continent, and we are people of the islands.

My life has occasionally carried me to the mainland, and there I have learned that pain and suffering and sacrifice, in a way that beggars all human explanation, are somehow a part of love's timeless format. I do not understand why. I only know, from my own experience, that it is so.

That is why romantic love, the beginning, sunlit island love between a man and a woman, is so incomplete as an ideal on which to establish our lives. Romantic love is based on promise, and the satisfaction of that promise. It is as if life employs romance to unite a man and a woman so that afterwards they can be plunged into the tides of wounding and disappointment and forgiveness which will wash them together toward the distant shore of that continent, where love in its fullness and vastness awaits their exploration.

I do not know the ending of the story I am about to tell you. The lovers are struggling singly in the water, pushing away from one another, being swept out from the shore which can be reached only when their efforts are united.

Terry and Anne fell in love and were married seventeen years ago. For Anne, Terry's promise was his confidence and his sensitivity, which augured in her mind a future of stability and intimacy. For Terry, Anne's promise was her loveliness and her sweet practicality, which raised in his mind an assurance of delights and comfort.

They set up house in Virginia, just across the Potomac from Washington, D.C. Terry secured a good job with the government and moved up rapidly in the ranks, drawing in time a handsome salary. A child came to Anne, then another, and a third, two girls and a boy. The long years of hard work, the routines and joys of family, both strengthened the young couple and drove wedges between them. The promises which each had envisioned when they went to the church for their marriage vows were, of course, not fully met, as they never are, and each felt disappointment grow, but their life together also brought them gifts which neither could have foreseen when they were young lovers. So they stayed together, raising their children, swallowing the disappointments along the way, and rejoicing when the good times were at hand.

The doctors told them that their fourth child would be a boy. This was perfect: two girls and two boys. Such a family was also, they felt, all that they could handle, and they agreed this would be their last child. Since Anne's delivery was to be by Cesarean section, they arranged with the doctor for Anne's fallopian tubes to be tied off once the birth had taken place.

Neither Anne nor Terry was truly prepared for what the operation would be like. Since, in this case, the doctors wanted Anne conscious, under local anesthetic, during the procedure, Terry accompanied her and stayed with her during the birth. He wanted to be with her; she wanted him there. Terry held his wife's hand and made himself watch as the scalpel made the incision. The surgical team peeled back the layers of flesh in the hump on Anne's stomach as the young husband stared.

Terry held on to Anne's fingers as the procedure unfolded. The doctor reached down and took out the birth sac, handing the little body to the pediatrician. Despite the blood and the mess and the impersonality of it all, Terry and Anne felt a thrill run through them. Their son, Philip his name would be, was coming into the world, and they squeezed one another's hands at the strangeness and joy of it all.

I don't know whether Terry or Anne was the first to discern that something was wrong. Probably, their first alarm came from the tone of the pediatrician's voice, or the stiffness of his body as he made his observations on the child for the record. Perhaps the young parents picked up that team members even behind their masks were showing themselves aghast as they regarded the little figure both doctors were now holding between them.

"Fingers: webbed. Toes: webbed. Ears: bulbous, displaced on the side of the head. Biceps: atrophied. Triceps: atrophied. Longissimus dorsi: atrophied. The muscles are just not there. He must have a diaphragm because he's breathing, but in the extremities there's almost no muscle tissue."

Terry looked down at Anne's head on the pillow. Her eyes squeezed shut and then opened wide, searching his face. Terry was aware that the surgeon was beside him, questioning him insistently.

"We cannot wait any longer. Do you want us to tie the tubes?"

Terry and Anne could not answer a word, could not assimilate what was going on. The pediatrician was reeling off more defects in Philip. The surgeon beside them at the head of the surgical gurney continued to insist.

"You must decide. We cannot wait. Do you want us to tie the tubes?"

"The whole thing was brutal," Terry whispered when he told me about it years later.

A kind nurse came to their rescue. "It's not a time to make permanent decisions," she gently advised. The doctor glared at her for the intrusion, and set the team to work closing Anne up.

In the days that followed, Terry and Anne visited their new son through the glass of the nursery. He lay in an incubator. His tiny body bristled with tubes, and he was swaddled in bandages. The womb had dealt monstrously with him. It was as if in the plate tectonics of gestation, his ears had erupted rather than merely formed and had drifted down the side of his head in a tiny geological cataclysm. Nature had forgotten most of his skeletal muscle.

To crown nature's spite, she suggested in his fingers and toes more reptile or duck than human being. His pathetic countenance was that of a hundred year old man. He labored in his breathing and twitched.

The doctors and other medical personnel helped as much as they could. Philip was transferred to Children's Hospital in downtown Washington. His birth defects were massive and probably terminal, but the doctors did not know for sure what was going to happen. None of them had ever seen a condition like this before. Philip was fed through tubes and continued to survive. Children's Hospital broadcast a national plea for information, and received word back that an Oregon doctor had published a paper on something like what had happened to Philip. His article was disappointing, merely informing them that such natal disaster was not entirely unique. He could not help the Children's Hospital doctors answer the parents' questions: How long would Philip live? Would he have a mind? What awaited them and their son?

Finally, the time came for Anne and Terry to take their baby home, and they entered a way of life they could never have dreamed about when they first fell in love, could never even have had nightmares about.

In many ways, their first task with Philip was to get to know him. They did this the way all parents do: by feeding him, changing him, talking to him, holding him when he cried. They tended Philip as tenderly as they had taken care of their other babies, but they had to accustom themselves to an almost total lack of response on his part. Locked in the world of his own tiny, limited, misfiring brain, he had no way to incorporate stimuli from without himself, or as the months advanced, to shine out love or gratitude to those who cared for him. They had no sign that he really knew they existed, or was accumulating any memory of them from one day to another. There was no firm indication that he even knew he existed.

But with all the defects that had accompanied him into life, he was a baby with baby needs and baby satisfactions, of food or bath or being changed, and meeting these needs, giving these satisfactions to his little scrap of life, acted on the young parents' hearts and drew them to him, though they never received the reward of a single glint of recognition from his eyes. Yet their determination strengthened with every day's passing to give their son the meager best which, under the circumstances, life had to offer him.

The difference for them, from other parents, from their experience with their other children, was that they knew he would die. No doctor could tell them when the end might come, only that it would, that he would never survive infancy.

Late one night Philip began convulsing and vomiting. He was gasping and struggling, turning blue. Panicked that he would die under their eyes, they called an ambulance and rushed him to Children's Hospital. This was their first crisis at home with Philip.

There were to be many more such crises. They became, in fact, seasoned veterans of crisis. Soon, they stopped using the ambulance service. If Philip went into crisis during the day, Anne would take him in the car to Children's, or, if Philip's symptoms were especially alarming, to nearby Fairfax County Hospital, where emergency room personnel could stabilize Philip until he was transported to Children's. If the crisis came upon them at night, Terry would be the carrier.

The alarms came thick and fast, and every time that the little baby pulled through, their hearts were bound tighter and tighter to him.

There was even a period when Anne and Terry allowed themselves briefly to hope that Philip might fool the experts, and live. After all, the doctors had no evidence, no previous case histories on which to base their opinion that Philip was doomed. Might not a parent's heart be as reliable about the future as an ignorant doctor's guess?

"I suppose I was a fool in some ways," Terry muses now. "Once a doctor was telling me Philip's kidneys were failing, and I couldn't stand it. I burst out, 'Keep him alive! Do a kidney transplant if necessary!' The doctor gazed at me for a moment. 'That would be cruel,' he answered me."

I don't think that either Terry or Anne could today explain to anyone how their love for Philip grew so deep. Terry tried to illustrate it for me by telling me about the one time Philip almost stood up. Terry was sitting on the couch with him, dandling him by his little hands. Philip's tiny, misformed feet rested on Terry's thighs. All of a sudden the baby stretched and stiffened his legs. For an instant, the little boy actually was standing, his weight on his own legs. A look of astonishment came over his wizened face. Terry's heart leaped; pride and hope were wild within him for a split second. Then Philip pitched over to the side, collapsing and vomiting from the strain and effort he had just expended.

"It was from this moment on," Terry said, "that I knew that there was no hope, that he was going to die."

The life they were leading took a tremendous toll on both parents. Terry was out frequently at night, hurrying across the Potomac, watching the lights on his dashboard clock register two A.M., three A.M., four or five A.M. When Philip was kept at the hospital, Anne stayed with him as much as possible, finding baby-sitters or swapping time with Terry. No schedule, no firm planning was possible. They both tried to make sure that their other three children had plenty of attention, but it was an impossible situation. Terry, often, was out on his feet at work.

As time went on, they became familiar regulars at Children's Hospital. They discovered an entire subculture they never knew existed, that of parents and children in acute distress. By sharing rooms and wandering the halls as they waited on treatment, they met children with cancer, with paralysis, with terrible systemic failures, with birth defects that tore their hearts.

Rebecca, a little girl with long red hair, became one of Anne's favorites. Anne appeared at the hospital one day with a set of bright combs in her own dark hair. She saw Rebecca staring, enthralled, at the comb set. Anne slowly disengaged the combs and let her hair fall. She extended them to Rebecca. The little girl's face shown bright as the sun as Anne showed her how to arrange them in her own red cascades.

Terry's favorite was a little boy with no arms or legs. He was spunky and brimming with charm. Terry smiled at the way he ordered the indulgent nuns around when they weren't quick enough to suit him.

The society of unfortunates in the hospital became, for a time, their group, one with whom they could share things they could share with no one else. Misfortune seemed to breed love.

Love, as it does, however, occasionally exacted its cost.

One morning Terry and Anne lingered over the breakfast table at their home. Anne was reading the newspaper. Terry was occupied with his own thoughts when, all of a sudden, Anne burst out wailing, a high-pitched shriek. He leapt to his feet. She dropped the newspaper and, in agony, buried her face in her hands. He looked down. She had been reading the obituaries.

"Rebecca is dead! Rebecca is dead!" she wailed over and over, as Terry stood frozen.

Fifteen months after Philip's birth, the last crisis of his life finally came in the early hours before dawn. Terry was the one who drove him to Children's Hospital. The receptionist knew him and directed him straight into an emergency treatment room to await the emergency team, which was busy with another child. Terry had virtually no feelings. He was numb, depleted by the months of hope and despair, of sleeplessness and unending exertion. He knew this was probably the last time he would be there with his son.

He lay Philip down on the metal table and stood behind his son's head watching him. Philip's poor mind could not process much of the world, but he had learned, somewhere down deep in his system, that being on tables like this meant that drastic, sometimes painful, treatments were going to be administered. Terry could see that the tiny boy was tense, as stiff as his muscle-less little limbs would let him be.

"I wanted to give him some peace," Terry said, "my last gift."

Terry began to massage the little forehead with his fingers, stroking gently from front to back. The expression on Philip's face changed. He suddenly relaxed and went limp, like a cat being petted.

"He would have purred if he had known how to purr. He was like people getting their back scratched, who keep on saying, 'Oh, that feels so good! Keep on! Don't stop. Keep on!'"

It was one of the strongest, most human reactions Terry had ever seen in his son. A long time went by, or so it seemed to Terry. He kept on stroking, but he was ready to drop over from fatigue.

A movement in the half lit room caught his attention. Against the far wall, a dark figure he had not noticed before was sitting in a chair, watching him. Slowly, the figure slid out of the chair and dropped to the floor. It was a woman, and she was silently crawling toward him. Terry was so drained he did not even ask himself what was going on. He regarded her incuriously as she came toward him and Philip. She rose slowly and stood beside him at the head of the table. Her fingers came over his, and she began to stroke Philip's forehead in exactly the same way he had been doing. With no word, she motioned him to lie down on a gurney against the other wall. Terry, woodenly, obeyed. Possibly, he is not sure, he drifted off quickly. Philip continued his silent purring, never knowing Terry was not behind him, which was probably what the dark figure intended.

At some point, a wheelchair was brought. They put Terry in it, with Philip on his knees.

"I remember the dark figure behind me, pushing the chair. I never found out who she was. She was like a strange miracle to me, an angel you take for granted."

Anne went over to the hospital the next morning while Terry stayed home with the other three children. The phone rang. It was Anne. "He's gone."

Terry called the baby-sitter and his mother. An hour or so later he walked into Philip's hospital room. A priest, a nun, and a nurse were standing awkwardly beside Anne. She was seated primly in a chair, her dead baby in her lap. She had refused to give up Philip.

Terry was inexpressibly weary. He went over to Anne and reached down for Philip. "Let me take him," he asked his wife gently.

"Get the hell away from me!" Anne hissed, holding on tight to Philip. Her eyes were wild with grief, like an uncomprehending tigress cuddling her dead cub.

Terry backed off, not knowing what to do. Anne talked for a while, Philip on her lap, and the four of them listened quietly to her.

After a while, Terry went back to her.

"The kids at home need us," he said softly. Anne looked at him. She knew she had to let go. Still as a statue, she let Terry lift Philip off her lap. He placed their son on the hospital bed, and took her home.

Philip's funeral took place in Zion Springs Cemetery, in Piedmont County, North Carolina. Terry, usually undemonstrative, wept inconsolably in the days before the funeral. Anne was in shock, tearless. She looked at her weeping husband as if he were a stranger. At the end of the funeral, she finally broke down, and Terry had to help her tear herself away from the little white casket so it could be lowered into the earth.

Things were not the same when they returned to Washington. Bitter memories ate at them. Terry gave up his job, to Anne's dismay, and they relocated back to Shelby. Each, in time, began to drift away from the other. Nowadays, they seldom talk. They live in the same house, but their love has vanished. Terry is frightened of the rage that he sees growing toward him in his wife. She has lost her respect for his promise, and is perfunctorily civil to him in their marriage, the way we sometimes are to those whom we regard as despicable. Their three older children are growing, and they have another son, Tommy, who was the first baby Anne held after the death of Philip. The children do their growing in a house that is, in so many ways that matter, silent.

As I said at the beginning, I do not as yet know the end of this story of Anne and Terry. Theirs is, unquestionably, a love story, at this point, the story of a love which grew cold and has now frozen over. The heroic capacities for love which Philip demonstrated that they possess are in ruins when they turn toward one another, as on rare occasions they do.

When their lives are over, what part will Philip have played in their destiny? If you believe in God, as Jesus represented Him, then you have to believe in mission, in a plan and a place for every creature, however small. In the vast schemes of God's love, what was Philip's mission, in his brief time of martyrdom among us? Anne and Terry will one day, we are promised, see Philip as he is, not as he appeared in that monstrous accident that cloaked his soul while he was among us, and they will, at long last, know.

"Well done!" they will hear, and Philip will applaud, his webbed hands as honored and lovely as those nail scarred ones of His Master, who came to command us to love, as Anne and Terry did, the Philips of this world.

Love is a continent and we are island people. Anne and Terry are struggling singly in the water, pushing away from one another, being swept out from the shore which can only be reached when their efforts are united.

Mildred's Glory

As I begin this page, a friend of mine, Mildred, has died, and I have just returned from her funeral.

My friend had been blessed with good health most of her life. Even at 76 she walked three miles a day. And how she walked! She would circle the plaza which surrounded the apartment building for the elderly where she lived. After a few turns to warm up, she would take the elevator up to the top of the building and climb down thirteen stories to the ground. Then she would repeat the exercise. She stayed in the pink of health.

When Mildred was young she must have been quite lovely, and as an aging woman she was still interested in clothes and make-up. Her pleasant face wore an expression of well-being, and she smiled readily. If you had seen her strolling in the mall near her home, you would have probably considered her an attractive lady. "Very classy," you might well have said to yourself.

Mildred loved the God of Glory and she loved her four grown children. These two loves marked the later years of her life.

The pair of loves was also a source of substantial pain to her. Two of her sons scorned Christianity and would not under any circumstances darken the door of a church. Mildred for years determined to correct this rejection by her offspring of Christ's Body, but nothing she tried was successful. She genuinely feared that only half her family would wind up in heaven with her.

In January of this year, she began to feel tired and weak. The doctors relieved her mind, declaring a thyroid deficiency. The treatments seemed slow in taking effect. By July it was obvious that something was going on that thyroid boosters could not heal. More extensive tests were ordered.

On July 20 the doctor's office called and asked her to come in to hear the results of the tests. The nurse on the phone was ominously specific: "Bring your daughter with you."

Mildred was informed that she had cancer in one of her lungs. The malignancy had already colonized her bones and was scattered all over her body. Her condition was hopeless. With treatments she might extend her life a few months, but the therapy would be drastic.

Mildred, classy lady, decided to forego treatment.

We human beings are image-making creatures. The number and quality of our images are what distinguish our minds from the simpler mental worlds of the animals which surround us.

We know something of the images with which Mildred's mind teemed in the exactly seven weeks of existence which remained to her. Her mind was peopled with images of glory and images of salvation.

A person who had loved order and planning all her life, Mildred mapped out carefully how she wished to spend those last weeks. She would not go into the hospital. She would stay as long as possible in her apartment close to her many friends. Her children and her pastor could come see her, but she did not wish to squander precious time with mere inquirers and acquaintances. Once she became bedridden, she projected, she would go to her daughter's home and die there.

She planned the final arrangements minutely, enclosing all her meticulous plans in one exceedingly well organized folder which had one objective, that of using glory to bring God and His wayward children together.

Mildred had had much experience of death. She was a widow and had observed in her husband and countless friends the acute agony that almost always accompanies the dissolution of the body. She recognized that death appears to those left living to be a vast blackness, like the turning out of all light, and that we know nothing definite of that apparent emptiness which awaits us, except that it is everlasting, that those who go into it do not return. Ever. Mildred never indulged herself in illusions about the horrific countenance of death. Death's face and her memories were her closest companions all during her last days and in the frequent awakenings she endured in the long nights.

Mildred had been privileged with what is called a full life. She had taken care of a husband and raised a family. She had worked at various jobs. She realized that she had often fallen short of her own ideals in her life, but she had learned to face her failures of family, personal relationship, and religion unflinchingly. She was comfortable with the idea of God's judgment, approaching her end with a sustaining sense of having her accounts neatly balanced by Christ Himself.

Consequently, Mildred did not wrestle with her dread antagonist merely in her own strength or even her own qualities as a person. She was fortified by glory, and glory was her goal. People who had contact with her in her last period recognized that something extraordinary, even more extraordinary than death, was taking place.

Her chief source of perturbation was that two of her children did not have their accounts as balanced as her own.

The chief evidence of Mildred's state of mind is found in the papers contained in that neat folder. She left in it an envelope filled with cash for the opening of the grave. There were also letters and information for people who were especially important to her. The folder also shows that the funeral service itself stood out as an opportunity. She planned it from beginning to end. It was to be her last flourish of glory. She was even to use her dead body for glory's sake.

This lady who always dressed herself with such class left directions that she be interred with hose on, a detail of funerary dress not usually observed, since funeral directors know that no one who views the body ever sees the legs of the deceased. The dress she selected for the occasion was lovely pink linen. The casket was to remain open during the entire service so that no one attending was allowed to forget that a dead body was what the gathering was all about.

Too, she had always wanted to be a author. (When younger she had even written some verses called "Poor Man's Cadillac" [unpublished]). During her final days she set aside some of her precious time for writing poetry, composing verses which would be read as part of the funeral service. One poem was directed especially to her children. In her poetic work she was much influenced by the Psalms, which had across the years helped her hone her sense of glory. Shifts of point of view and the free mixing of pronouns (I, she, we, they) characterized Mildred's technique, as in the Psalmists. She gave the poem a title: "After I'm Gone."

The songs Mildred selected to be sung on either side of the reading of her farewell to her children were "Precious Memories" and "I Won't Have to Cross Jordan Alone."

Perhaps the clearest affirmation of Mildred's sense of glory and her desire to communicate it to others was her scheme for the funeral sermon itself. Raised in evangelical churches and steeped in gospel hymns, glory for Mildred meant not only good manners and thoughtfulness for others, elegant dresses, and creative writing, although all these things were involved in her intricate sense of glory. Glory also meant heaven, the home place of God, where no light is needed because the luminous Goodness emanating from the Godhead makes heaven the bright place human beings yearn for, the place Mildred anticipated so strongly as she endured the indignities of incontinence and barely controlled pain which were her doorway into the darkness.

She was quite eager for other people (especially those two lost sons) to be able to share the heavenly glory which would be hers.

So she chose her pastor, the Reverend Morris Bagwell, to deliver the funeral sermon. Her only instructions to him were, "Keep it short." She had no need to advise him closely in what she wanted. She knew him well and could calculate accurately what he would say in his sermon. He was an East Tennessee evangelistic preacher. She knew that he would waste little time eulogizing her life, which might disappoint her family a little. Rather, he would talk about glory and salvation and offer every person in the chapel the choice of sharing in the heaven she so firmly believed she was going to herself.

For Mildred recognized that the glory of heaven, like all glory, had to be chosen. Glory was not inevitable. It was option. Some members of her own family, her own children, had not chosen it. Reverend Bagwell would use her death not to rhapsodize about her life, but to try to draw others to contemplate the same destiny which she had so thoughtfully elected.

The night of the receiving and the funeral went like clockwork, just as Mildred had designed things. She lay in splendor for all to see. The crowd was substantial. There were laughter and tears in front of her open casket, exactly as she would have wished.

The first solo was sung, "Precious Memories," and the moment came for the reading of her moving farewell to her daughter and three sons. They sat on the front pew of the funeral chapel and gravely listened as her last good-bye was read to them. The closing lines to her children are especially revelatory of what her calculations were in the design of the service which would ceremonialize her passing:

"After I'm Gone"
Although God needed her in heaven
He knows we need her too.
He gives us peace through memories,
To comfort all our days
And lets us know she's with us still
In Oh! so many ways.
A smile, a touch, a word we speak,
Brings back sweet memories.
The tears we shed help ease our pain,
And we all agree,
That somewhere up in heaven,
Mama's watching and smiling too,
And some sweet day we'll meet again
Up there beyond the blue,
Her and my daddy too.
Love to all of you,
Mama

For the most part, her children listened stoically. It is certainly possible that two of them listened defensively, sensing the appeal that their mother had prepared for them, and perhaps still not fully aware of what her passing had withdrawn from their lives.

After the "I Won't Have to Cross Jordan Alone" solo, which expressed Mildred's own explanation for what people miscalled her courage as she faced death (she saw her strength not as courage but as purpose!), Pastor Bagwell did exactly what she had entrusted him to do.

His sermon text was "We don't sorrow like those who have no hope," and he used the quotation poetically, returning to it over and over again like a refrain, waving its banner of hope before the minds of those at the funeral who yearned for the capacity to live with eagerness no matter what came along in life, as Mildred had lived, even when what came along was death.

Mildred would have loved it. She would also have been pleased that her last flourish of glory had been brought about just as she had so carefully planned. A remarkable performance—that was what her life had been from the instant she heard the doctor pronounce her dreadful doom until the final moment of her obsequies.

Mildred was, of course, not a theologian. She probably had never even troubled to define glory because she knew so well to her own satisfaction what it was. Glory was light, it was a beacon, it was supernatural grace mixed into the commonplaceness of life. Glory was the "Well done!" which she tremulously awaited, pronounced by the lips of the LORD of Glory Himself to her, to Mildred in her white robe, from His glistening throne. Glory for Mildred was sanctuary against pain, against meaninglessness, and against the darkness of extinction.

"Yea, though I walk through the valley of the shadow of death...," Mildred had read a thousand times. And in the end, glory had sustained her.

How had this lady in pink, like David the King three thousand years ahead of her, come to discover the precious power and consolation of glory? How had a relatively untutored woman found such rare sustenance for her living and her dying?

The answer is that glory shines in a timeless and noble tradition to which all humankind has equal access, from highborn emperors to humble souls like Mildred. Mildred did not concoct out of her own twentieth century American mind the forms of glory which so strengthened her as she lived and died. She had discovered glory in a medium of texts and stories which were utterly natural to the spiritual environment which gave her spiritual birth. In her case, glory was mediated through the Psalms and the Gospels, the accounts in Exodus and the word music of Isaiah, as well as through hymns and popular religious literature. It came to her through sermons and Sunday School lessons. Her sense of glory took shape not through the spirit of novelty and happenstance which reigned in the secular world around her, but through a well defined tradition of reading and listening, of sacred song and worship.

Mildred believed that anyone could apprehend glory if they chose to do so, and in the same ways she had apprehended it, through the traditions of Christ's Body, the church. Those traditions which she had imbibed so deeply were, she knew from her own family's experience, vanishing from many lives because people like her sons chose to scorn them or at least chose not to honor them.

Because such people would not attend to glory themselves, Mildred decided to take glory to them in her last moments under the sun.

Put in another way, she knew that her sons would never voluntarily attend church, where they might encounter glory. But they would, she was certain, attend their mother's funeral. Calculatingly, and probably with a certain amount of glee, she administered a dose of glory to them in the same motherly way she had spooned out tonic to her brood when they were young.

Mildred's two sons and all the other rejecters of glory who had attended her final rites walked out of the funeral home apparently unconverted and possibly breathed a sigh of relief that they were still safe in their heathenism. This would not have surprised the classy (and crafty) lady at all.

She was confident that traces of the glory she had been vouchsafed would linger on in the minds of all who knew her and who had come to witness glory's final flourishes from her life.

Time will tell whether her gambit for glory will bring the prizes she in her last act set out to capture.

Time will tell whether that poem she penned was prophetic:

> *...somewhere up in heaven*
> *Momma's watching and smiling too,*
> *And some sweet day we'll meet again,*
> *Up there beyond the blue....*

❦❦❦❦

Epilogue to the Eloquence of God

"What happened after that night?" Thomas Cameron had asked me at the airport (see "Aftermath" in Part One), and I was not able to respond adequately, or better said, chose not to attempt a response which I was certain would in the circumstances be inadequate.

I could have answered, "I was called toward the Gospel, toward the Dream of God," but such an expository reply would have told him nothing significant. The Gospel is probably incommunicable without the mode of story.

The vision which contains the narratives I have included in this volume is what I would like to have given Thomas in answer to his question, the vision of God's unceasing and idiomatic appeal to His children through event and circumstance. But I knew it would be impossible to express that vision to him in a few words. So—wisely, I now think—I stayed silent.

And then I went home and continued work on this book.

"Jesus Saves" read the signs along back roads of the South. "Are you saved?" is a common question from evangelists who buttonhole us on the sidewalks around the Squares in Appalachian towns.

What happened subsequent to that night was that after many, many years, I arrived at the conclusion that both the sign, "Jesus Saves," and the question, "Are you saved?" are ineloquent, in the sense in which I had learned that God is eloquent. Such approaches are almost a sanction to continue the self-centeredness which so torments humankind, whereas Jesus Christ through the Gospel invites us to the risk and perhaps even the death of our self.

God's eloquence is functional. Its purpose is not to beguile us. Its purpose is not limited to tempting us toward heaven. Its purpose is to draw us toward the Gospel, which, while it deals with both heaven and salvation, is much more than the mere consolation which certain sectors of the Christian establishment have marketed for the past two hundred years. God's eloquence appeals to our sense of adventure, not our sense of safety. His eloquence appeals to our capacity to dare, not to our jaded sense of weariness with the failing world. The Gospel is a challenge to wake up, to spring into action, to take part in a massive, perilous, time spanning campaign against death, against suffering, and against sin. The Gospel is a set of marching orders, a clear delineation of strategy in an all consuming war effort, a call to sacrifice and glory. The Gospel is the promise of ultimate victory.

God's eloquence exercises our aspiration and our faith. It draws us toward joining Him in the adventure of realizing His dream.

Here ends Part Two of *To Dream Like God*, which displays what happens to an author once the moonsurf of glory flows over his imagination.

Here also ends Volume One of *To Dream Like God*.

Volume Two, Part Three, will feature accounts of how that imagination was honed, as a coward learns courage, a heart of stone is turned into a heart of flesh, and ignoble aspiration is transmuted into nobility.

Part Four will bring this entire series of spiritual quest to its successful conclusion when the narrator grasps the full meaning of Christ's promise to return to earth. Reality will be reconceived and refashioned, so that pain, anguish, sin and death no longer have any part in the world and human life.

Acknowledgments & Errata

I wish to acknowledge the use of the following materials in Volume One of To Dream Like God:

The poem used in "Mildred" was written by Mildred Vineyard and is used by permission of the executor of her estate, Robert Vineyard.

Errors: *Since I wrote this book, I have discovered one or two errors of fact in my text. One is that "Up Home" may not have burned down -- my Aunt Sarah's memory is that it was bulldozed. As best I recall, my mother told me about the house-burning. I do not know which version of Up Home's fate is true, but probably Aunt Sarah's is. A formidable memory is only one of her imposing virtues. Second, my recollection of Zion Springs Church is that it was constructed of wood and glistened white in the Sunday morning sun. Only when I saw the photographs at my Aunt Sarah's home recently did I realize that my memory was faulty: Zion Springs was of brick, although it did have white columns and the steps at one time were painted white, according to my aunt. Evidently, my little boy's mind retained the glowing white image and forgot the bricks. I deliberately leave the error in the text.*

Readers interested in seeing pictures of many of the people and places which appear in *To Dream Like God* (Amazonian scenes, Garlan and Helen, Sarah and Lowell, Mildred, Up Home, etc.) may do so by going to the book's website at:

www.todreamlikegod.com

INFORMATION ON ORDERING
COPIES OF
TO DREAM LIKE GOD

It is hoped that readers will give copies of this book to unbelieving friends (Volume One is especially recommended for this purpose) or to fellow believers who are seeking a closer relationship with the Lord. If your local bookshop does not carry *To Dream Like God*, copies of either Volume One or Volume Two or both volumes may be ordered in the following ways:

LAND MAIL:

L.B. May & Associates

3517 Neal Drive

Knoxville, Tennessee 37918

PHONE:

865-922-7495

(This is the office of the American Distributor of Wordsworth Classics)

VISA/MASTERCARD AND AMERICAN EXPRESS ACCEPTED

E-MAIL:

lbmay@tds.net

OR:

http://www.todreamlikegod.com

OR:

http://www.wordsworthclassics.com

VISA/MASTERCARD AND AMERICAN EXPRESS ACCEPTED

March 14, 2004

TO: David Morgan, COADVICE
        Mumbles
        Swansea, Wales, UK

You asked me to let you know how publication and promotional plans for my book are progressing. Right now Mary B. and I plan (this is very much a family enterprise) to publish this collection of true stories in two user-friendly volumes (divided into four parts), rather than as one super-fat book.

Volume One, Part One opens with the story of the atheist who comes to believe in God, the same story which you read and gave in manuscript form to your agnostic friend Tina. (By the way, has she made progress in her quest to believe in God? What an impressive believer she will make if she comes to Christ!) I think the "Angels Laughed" piece is a great story of spiritual search (from my own life, as you know), and can be read with respect by even the most militant atheist. We plan Volume One to be about 160 pages and of a very reasonable cost so that this story (and the others in Part Two) can be given by Christians to unbelievers. We hope believers will purchase multiple copies to give away to people like we met in your home during the Alpha Course evenings last month, either seekers or those who have fallen away from the church.

Part Two of Volume One consists of six true stories of God's coming into the lives of people to encourage them and carry them toward the true Gospel. These stories are powerful, probably the best things the Lord has ever given me to write. I think they will be an eye-opener to unbelievers and a great encouragement to believers, especially believers who waver (don't we all?!), thinking they are out of touch with God, as our beloved Tom did. These accounts demonstrate that God is actually always there, active and on the move.

Volume Two is very different from the first volume. Part Three is a love story, showing how God uses the commonplaces of romance and marriage to draw the former atheist professor closer to Him. It also features accounts of how the professor is taught to cope with fear and dread, the two great plagues of his life, and how to aspire to the highest destiny possible for human beings, that of the Gospel of Christ. I know I look a little dumb and bumbling in these accounts, but they really happened and show how God can use even a mistake-prone, misfiring brain like mine to speak to His children.

Part Four will carry the entire series of spiritual quest to its successful outcome. This concluding section features a haunting Civil War story, that of my great-great grandfather Malcom, as well as the story of Perpetua, that astonishing young woman who battled her way to sainthood in the Carthage arena in 203 AD. These stories are blended into my own, showing how the glory of Christ's final Victory is displayed to the one-time atheist and how his life bursts into fulfillment as he is commissioned to play a tiny but momentous role in hastening this Victory.

The entire series is crowned with the very last section of the second volume (called "Embarkation"), which shows how Christ's Victory is not just a moment of emotional triumph, but stunningly practical, a coordinate that the narrator can use to shape his own life in a radical way. The narrator is shown that Christ's Victory means that all reality will be reconceived and refashioned so that pain, anguish, sin and death no longer have any part in the World and human life. The narrator sees Christ's return as an utterly unique aspect of the Gospel which is often unduly downplayed by both believers and unbelievers.

David, each of the volumes stands alone and can be read individually, but Mary and I hope that readers who encounter one volume will be enticed to pick up the other one, so that they can get the full effect of the entire spiritual-quest series. Each of the four parts has its own title, but the entire series will go by the name TO DREAM LIKE GOD, the theme that ties the four parts (and the events of my own life) together.

David, my kind of writing, I know, is not for everyone, but there is a huge literate reading public of questing believers and unbelievers out there, and this work was composed for just such. The main idea is to appeal to unbelievers and to strengthen believers, the same process which has operated in my own life.

Thanks for your advice and counsel in this project. Let me know if you think this two volume, four part plan will carry out our purposes.

Yulan